# Musicians' Migratory Patterns

*Musicians' Migratory Patterns: The African Drum as Symbol in Early America* questions the ban that was placed on the African drum in early America. It shows the functional use of the drum for celebrations, weddings, funerals, religious ceremonies, and nonviolent communication. The assumption that "drums and horns" were used to communicate in slave revolts is undone in this study. Rather, this volume seeks to consider the "social place" of the drum for both blacks and whites of the time, using the writings of Europeans and colonial-era Americans, the accounts of African American free persons and slaves, the period instruments, and illustrations of paintings and sculpture.

The image of the drum was effectively appropriated by Europeans and Americans who wrote about African American culture, particularly in the nineteenth century, and re-appropriated by African American poets and painters in the early twentieth century who recreated a positive nationalist view of their African past. Throughout human history, cultural objects have been banned by one group to be used by another, objects that include books, religious artifacts, and ways of dress. This study unlocks a metaphor that is at the root of racial bias—the idea of what is primitive—while offering a fresh approach by promoting the construct of multiple-points-of-view for this social-historical presentation.

**Christopher Johnson** was a research fellow at the W. E. B. Du Bois Institute for Afro-American Research at Harvard University. He served on the faculty of the Institute for Doctoral Studies in the Visual Arts (IDSVA), Portland, Maine, and the Eugene Lang College of Liberal Arts at the New School in Manhattan.

**CMS Cultural Expressions in Music**
Series Editor: Franco Sciannameo
*Carnegie Mellon University*

Created in 2009, ***Cultural Expressions in Music*** began as a series of monographs that sought to promote and share the diversity of perspectives, cultures, experiences, philosophies, and contributions of The College Music Society's membership and the music community at large. The volumes published under this rubric follow the tenets of geo-musicology, an interdisciplinary outreach of recent coinage, which integrates musical expression, geo-political thinking, and migratory movement of musicians, musical genres, styles, repertoire, and practices. The monographs and edited collections in the series urge readers worldwide to reflect, musically and culturally, upon one of the most pressing issues of our time: immigration.

**Musicians' Migratory Patterns**
The American-Mexican Border
*Mauricio Rodriguez*

**Musicians' Migratory Patterns**
The African Drum as Symbol in Early America
*Christopher Johnson*

**Musicians' Migratory Patterns**
The Adriatic Coasts
*Edited by Franco Sciannameo*

# Musicians' Migratory Patterns

## The African Drum as Symbol in Early America

**Christopher Johnson**

NEW YORK AND LONDON

First published 2020
by Routledge
605 Third Avenue, New York, NY 10017

and by Routledge
2 Park Square, Milton Park, Abingdon, Oxon, OX14 4RN

First issued in paperback 2021

*Routledge is an imprint of the Taylor & Francis Group, an informa business*



Publisher's Note
The publisher has gone to great lengths to ensure the quality of this reprint but points out that some imperfections in the original copies may be apparent.

*Library of Congress Cataloging-in-Publication Data*
Names: Johnson, Christopher (Professor of Culture and Media), author.
Title: Musicians' migratory patterns : the African drum as symbol in early America / Christopher Johnson.
Description: New York : Routledge, 2019. | Includes index.
Identifiers: LCCN 2018059741 (print) | LCCN 2019000720 (ebook) | ISBN 9780429027512 (ebook) | ISBN 9780367136260 (hardback)
Subjects: LCSH: African Americans—Music—History and criticism. | Drum—Social aspects—America—History. | Music and race—United States—History.
Classification: LCC ML3556 (ebook) | LCC ML3556 .J64 2019 (print) | DDC 786.9089/96073—dc23
LC record available at https://lccn.loc.gov/2018059741

ISBN 13: 978-1-03-224009-1 (pbk)
ISBN 13: 978-0-367-13626-0 (hbk)

DOI: 10.4324/9780429027512

Typeset in Times New Roman
by Apex CoVantage, LLC

**I dedicate this work to the efforts of the chroniclers of the African experience in the Americas who over the centuries saw a uniqueness worthy of preserving for our time.**

# Contents

# Illustrations

# Preface

Customarily, a book's authors or editors expect an authoritative figure in their field of inquiry to write a preface to their works in the form of a philosophical summation that also endorses its contribution to scholarly discourse.

Christopher Johnson did not have a chance to fulfill that expectation. Sadly, he died August 5, 2019, from kidney failure as a result of an extended and courageous battle with prostate cancer. Researching, writing, and lecturing about the role of the African drum as a symbol of early America was Christopher's passion for decades. He shared his vision with his beloved wife Wendy Joseph, family members, colleagues, and students. Finally, he also proposed the publication of his findings to The College Music Society's Series *Monographs & Bibliographies in American Music* and its series editor Professor Michael J. Budds from the University of Missouri.

Michael and Christopher conceived an initial plan and began working in earnest. Unfortunately, their effort was interrupted by Christopher's health challenges. Thankfully, following a remission, he was able to resume the work under my editorship on behalf of the College Music Society's series *Cultural Expressions in Music—Musicians' Migratory Patterns* published by Routledge. Regrettably, our work together was also interrupted by the author's recurring illness.

*The African Drum as Symbol of Early America* is being published posthumously based on the restructuring of the text Christopher Johnson and I agreed upon. It consists of an introduction, four chapters, and an epilogue, in addition to bibliographic information and an index.

In the course of our correspondence, Christopher communicated to me that

> this project represents the first scholarly attempt to give meaning to the commonly held belief that the African drum was banned during slavery. It is a cliché in the study of American history that throughout the

slave epoch the drum was feared by slave owners because of its potential use as an instrument of communication for revolts. The drum as well as "other loud instruments" were prohibited due to their perceived connection with violence. My interest has been to assemble documentary evidence and consider the myth and reality of the African drum in America from colonial times to the turn of the twentieth century. My intent is to take the idea of the African hand drum and trace it—pull it—through time to our day.

Chapter One is an assessment, over time, of those commentators who have shaped the record of the past on this subject. As the collection of accounts grew in number during my research, I was taken by the almost eccentric array of whites—American and European, women and men—who found African American culture interesting enough to write about it, notate its music, or make drawings. I have always been fascinated by the relationship between the viewers and the viewed, particularly in the realm of cultural difference. Taking into account the lack of understanding on the part of the white observer witnessing black culture, a deficit that they often readily admitted, I believe that it is important to begin with a discussion of this group.

Chapter Two is a presentation of accounts that focus on performance practices—how African Americans sang, danced, and played music that involved the drum and on which occasions. These descriptions document African-styled instruments and ways of playing but also suggest the New World influences that allowed for the mix of European clothing, dances, and instruments that evolved alongside African ways.

Chapter Three details a chronology of those accounts, beginning in the colonial era, one that describes the prohibition of the drum. The issues of slave revolts, communication, and phases of acculturation are considered here—along with the observations of whites, contributors to the Slave Narrative Collection commented on the place of the drum in slave society. The narratives reveal a variety of activities with which the drum is rarely associated.

Chapter Four presents the concept of surrogates, what came to replace the drum where it was prohibited, and how song, dance, and the performance of other musical instruments compensated for the missing drum. In this chapter, I also consider the shout and the religious ring dance and their connection to rhythmic practices.

The Epilogue concludes that a hierarchical view of culture has, over time, had an effect on how the West has valued people's practices. As a force, modernism's primitive bent, beginning at the dawn of the twentieth century, began to value the art of tribal cultures as containing elements equally expressive yet unusual to Europe. Primitivism sought an

> alternative aesthetic, although as an artistic evolutionary path turned few of its discoveries into lasting concepts. The lament here is that non-Western cultures have been continually misconstrued. What I will call the "disconnect" of primitivism is that contiguous, changing, improvisatory ideas are presented as representative, fixed notions.

Christopher Johnson's book represents just a piece of his vast knowledge about African-American Studies, world-wide cultural issues, and performative aspects of drumming. Those fortunate to have been involved in bringing this work to fruition hope that it may stimulate others to continue deepening the scholarly path in African-American Studies Christopher so well realized. It was a dream and hope that inspired him to the last moment.

Franco Sciannameo

# Acknowledgments

On behalf of Christopher Johnson, I offer thanks to Wendy Joseph and to all those who were close to Christopher throughout the writing process. They include his colleagues at the Institute for Doctoral Studies in the Visual Arts (IDSVA), Portland, Maine, and the Eugene Lang College of Liberal Arts at the New School in Manhattan and his students who, no doubt, will carry his knowledge forward. Further, thanks are due to Michael J. Budds for his initial interest in Christopher's work and for forwarding the project to me as a great fit for the *Cultural Expressions in Music Series*. On my part, I thank the College Music Society's Board of Editors and Professor Todd Sullivan in particular for encouraging the ideas developed in the series. Also, I thank Professor Kenneth Keeling from the Carnegie Mellon School of Music for reading Christopher's latest draft and offering important suggestions. As well, Constance Ditzel, senior editor of music at Routledge, has been exceptional in guiding the project toward fruition, including the reshaping of its format to suit the new editorial vision for the series as a more agile, synthetic source of information.

Franco Sciannameo
August 2019
Pittsburgh, Pennsylvania

# Introduction

This project represents the first scholarly attempt to give meaning to the commonly held belief that the African drum was banned during slavery. It is a cliché in the study of American history that throughout the slave epoch the drum was feared by slave owners because of its potential use as an instrument of communication for revolts.[1] The drum as well as "other loud instruments" were prohibited due to their perceived connection with violence.[2] A greater symbolism has grown up around the image of the African savage and his drum. Mystery, not knowing the message of the drum, has served as a source of stereotyping. Added to this is the presumption that, whatever their practices, blacks must be simpleminded, brutal, and inferior. These three characterizations of violence, mystery, and inferiority cloud many considerations of the place of the drum in African and African American culture. In Africa the link to culture that the drum provides is there today, as it has always been. Because the drum was prohibited in America, there is a strong tension surrounding the historical treatment of this subject.

What was the outcome for the African American separated from this cultural reference? My interest has been to assemble documentary evidence and consider the myth and reality of the African drum in America from colonial times to the turn of the twentieth century. My intent is to take the idea of the African hand drum and trace it—pull it—through time to our day. To tell the story, this study presents (1) the recollections of observers, often American and European travelers; (2) the accounts of African Americans slaves, freemen, and former slaves; (3) physical evidence—actual drums and other instruments; and (4) illustrations and descriptions of drawings, paintings, newspapers, and magazines, where the idea of the drum is considered. The reflections of 140 different individuals are the source of this study, drawn from a database of 563 records that was three years in the making.

With these words, Christopher begins his passionate narrative about the migratory transit of the African drum to America.

The illustrations described in the text or suggested throughout feature nineteenth-century drawings of African Americans that were placed in books, magazines, and newspaper articles. These portrayals show a popularized image of the slave and former slave, often racist, and are useful today in showing the coexistence of Old World and New World customs and dress.

The basis for this study has been in part a group of anthologies in African American history.[3] The works of Lynne Emery,[4] Dena Epstein,[5] The Georgia Writers' Project, George Rawick, Eileen Southern,[6] and John Szwed,[7] originally published in the 1970s (except for The Georgia Writers' Project's 1940 piece and one of Eileen Southern's 1990 works), served as important sources for my citations. These authors had their own agendas for describing dance, song, and the conditions of the slave and African American music. They have all called attention to the drum as a vital part of African American culture. None were focused solely on the drum and their studies have not considered the opinions of white observers as such.[8] The present work represents an example of the transition in historical views from a consensus stereotype—the drum as exotica—to a revisionist definition—the drum as cultural component—to a social history model: the drum's relation to diverse groups at varying times for specific reasons. The scope of this study spans accounts from North America, the Caribbean, and Africa. This topic can only be understood within the context of the Americas as a whole.

## Firsts

There are a number of unique insights that surfaced from my analysis in the following pages. In Chapter One it becomes clear that the sheer variety of descriptions suggests an inconsistency in the idea that the drum was totally banned in North America and that African-like practices continued. Among the performance settings described by whites are drumming on slave ships, at weekend celebrations, during Christmas and New Year festivities, and at weddings and funerals. Benjamin Latrobe witnessed a dance scene in New Orleans in the early nineteenth century at which he estimated there were 600 participants. One historical match that I discovered while considering Latrobe's words was that one description of women dancing strikingly resembles a famous folk-art painting of a plantation scene attributed to the 1700s. In the painting as well as in his description the women hold white handkerchiefs, reminiscent of known African dance practices. The second chapter also credits the year 1580 with one of the earliest references in writing to African American drumming.

Chapter Three presents the surprising testimony of one former slave whose interview is found in *Drums and Shadows*.[9] She described how the names or circumstances of misbehaving young women in her Southern community were "put on the banjo." She compared this to what she had heard was formerly the practice among Africans in Africa. She was describing the onomatopoeic aspects of African American instrumental performance, imitating the voice and revealing that instruments talked to her and others from her home. Her story provides an example of a surrogate use of New World instruments for Old World purposes.

## Insights and Approaches

In spite of the fact that the life of the slave was mired by prohibitions, I have chosen the "glass is half full" approach; if cultural practices were allowed at all, then they would probably continue. Part of my objective in this project has been to take these accounts and enliven them, to cull from them, to uncover the spirit and truths that might reside in these transcriptions by reading closely and by attempting to understand the informants' words.

I have also been interested in utilizing these sources in a new way. This study represents an original interpretation of the resources that the older anthologies present to shape a single theme-based investigation. Sterling Stuckey, in fact, mentioned the potential use of these sources in his book *Going through the Storm: The Influence of African American Art in History* (1993), which itself represents an important interpretation of African American musical culture.[10] I am interested in the social place of the drum for both blacks and whites. I care equally for the viewers and the viewed. Although it might seem a contradiction to present a social history of an inanimate object, my purpose is to trace, by focusing on the drum, the contexts and cultural activities that were the brunt of so much restriction during slavery. A limitation, from the historian's point of view, is the relative rarity of the accounts and the need to view them across time and in far-ranging locales in order to create a narrative of value. I believe that by carefully framing the various references in time and considering them in a chronology, as I have done in each section, a strong story emerges in spite of the size or breadth of the sample.

Another starting place or approach for this study has been the question: If drums were banned, in what ways did the African rhythmic sense, so prevalent in twentieth-century African American music and culture, survive? I do not claim that for this question I have the answer. My point is that for this study I believe that I have a good question. I have been inspired by classic facts-first social history studies from totally unrelated fields whose authors have the courage to assemble the research and let it speak.

Such works as Mary Ryan's *Cradle of the Middle Class* (1983), a study of family and society in nineteenth-century upstate New York, and Patricia

Nelson Limerick's *The Legacy of Conquest* (1987), a consideration of "the conquerors" of the American West and how they became the victims, are both powerful pieces because they utilize multiple viewpoints.[11] Ryan described the male population, the female population, and the owners and workers as she portrayed the transition from preindustrial to early industrial existence. Limerick showed how, depending on the perspective, Native Americans, missionaries, land speculators, or farmers became both invader and victim. It is from these influences that I came to my research with the realization that this story is greater than just black history. *The African Drum as Symbol in Early America* is similarly a tale with more than one point of view.

## Background and Contexts

I have thought about what North America would have been like and would be like today if a ban on the African drum during the slave epoch had never happened. African Americans in the States would have been identified with drumming and possibly not with the spiritual or dance or jazz or soul or hip hop. Drumming would have been yet another hybrid, not like jazz, but something else. I carry this picture in my mind of a black man or woman carrying in a bag over the shoulder a djembe, that ubiquitous bowl-and-stem-shaped hand drum that is now very much a world music icon and a multicultural symbol. I see young African Americans everywhere with drums flung over their shoulders—a prop, a tool, a communicator of the African diaspora. Brazil has samba drums, Trinidad the steel drum. What if there were a North American drum? Well, there is a North American drum: in the 1920s, the jazz trap set emerged.[12]

But what if there had been no interruption, no surrogation, and African Americans walked the streets with drums, placed them in their homes, and used them in this central sense as the peoples of Africa do? Then, African Americans would not be American, could be one response. More importantly, this symbol could have become an even more fundamental identifier of American culture than, for instance, apple pie. The African drum, nonetheless, was destined to be banned because it was un-American. Literally and figuratively, the drum represented cultural baggage. European instruments were privileged; African American hybrids, such as the banjo, were invented. It remains an important reality that such resistance to the Old World helped shape the New.

What does it mean for a people to lose their timekeeper, their rhythm maker, and their sense of time and to be forced to do without, to hide, and to improvise alternatives? My view is that the suppression and omission led to solutions that have since reshaped world music. Had Africans arrived in the Americas as free or contract labor, like the immigrants from Ireland, Italy, or later Southeastern Europe, the drum might have accompanied them. What a different world this would have been. The reality is that African, Asian, and East Indian peoples were bound laborers in the Americas. Cultural objects were few. The iconography of the Americas became European-based. Native American culture Americanized everyone via the symbolism of the warrior, for example. Food crops such as maize and the idea of boundless freedom became cliché for the indigenous. Their cultural objects and their drum, especially, represented primitive America, the American past. Although it may be stripped away, culture remains in us through our actions. Culture is practice. Although the drum was taken from African slaves, their customs remained in language, religion, and the physical crafts that African Americans performed in the New World, from boat making and ironwork to agricultural methods and building construction techniques.[13]

## Social Communication

Of the numerous varieties of African drums, most are made to be played out-of-doors. By design, a drum is meant to be heard from far away. From close range the musical instrument can be loud and penetrating, deafening, not like a book or a liturgy. A drum is a novel social communicator. Drumming calls for a response, an action, a song, a dance. The idea of the war drum is a narrow notion, a functional and inspirational use, and this only. The martial in drumming is a reality, nonetheless: the drum roll commands attention in a primal sort of way, whether heard in the context of a marching band or delivered by a performer in a jazz club. The fact that in North America drums for the out-of-doors came indoors is an important point of social history. The Western classical orchestra favors timpani, which are big drums, and other powerful percussion in a symphonic stage setting. The instruments that make up the jazz trap set, however, are taken strictly from the field band. What does it mean that America took to hot, loud drumming?

In the early twentieth century Americans became primal via jazz and African American culture. The industrial age ushered in, instigated, inspired, and approved of noise on an unprecedented scale. The sonic dimension of this practice of the loud sound is what was new. The microphone, the phonograph, the big band all turned up the volume in American culture. Not absurdly, jazz was the music of drums and horns inside a room! David Nye observed that, beginning in the late nineteenth century, urban Americans sought release in public dance halls and in such leisure time pursuits as "spieling," literally a spinning dance.[14] Loud and aggressive cities made for loud and aggressive entertainment. Arguably, twentieth-century music can be tracked as evolving and increasing toward distortion, always trying to become larger than itself. Radio and movies are not only potentially loud but broad and wide in terms of their reach—further than any drum. The electric guitar, first in African American music and later in white rock and roll, made noise and distorted a part of the musical language. Acoustic blues artist Robert Johnson, in the mid-1930s, slapped and stopped the strings on his guitar percussively and bent and "ghosted" notes (suggested pitches without playing them, for example, by not finishing a musical phrase) in a way that Jimi Hendrix did later in the 1960s, utilizing the electric guitar's feedback capabilities.[15] Champions of avant garde jazz from the 1960s on and, most recently, of hip hop music have made their own contributions to both the increase in volume and distortion in musical culture. This line of thinking quickly leads to a recognition of the postmodern in the arts, the sampling—I mean both borrowing from and copying—and the expanding of ideas of previous practitioners.

We have been conquered by sound. Music from far away has not only reached us but synchronized us in the form of handheld personal digital devices. We internalize, hear in our heads, and possibly feel less of the once body-held vibrations of physical sound. Benjamin Latrobe, writing in the early nineteenth century, felt the drumming of Congo Square in New Orleans through his feet and began a search for the source of this sound.[16] Early Americans reacted to this notion of the feeling of black sound by banning it. What eventually emerged from African American culture are hybrids based in song form—the spirituals, the blues, and instrumental interpretations of popular songs—that utilized European instruments in new ways. To return to the metaphor, in the early twentieth century black drumming returned via jazz. Rhythm moved indoors during the industrial age and, then, in the digital age, inside each of us. It is then essential to return to an earlier America to consider the dynamic—the politic—of culture and sound relationships.

It is possible that my drum dream has already occurred in reality in versions of the portable sound system. The new Congo Square may be the iPhone-powered silent rave in Manhattan's Union Square! In the preface to Ralph Ellison's *Invisible Man* (1952), the narrator wants to play Louis Armstrong's rendition of "What Did I Do to Be So Black and Blue" on many phonographs and to imagine that there would have been no way to "sync" each "track."[17] The "record player" was, indeed, an earlier portable music player for the masses, a box with a handle. The portable digital device linked to a satellite network plays and sends music far beyond the scope of earlier means. The digital device does not make music; it merely plays it. We have nearly infinite power to communicate and to play recordings, but the drum as an acoustic instrument creates sound. We are not performers of sound but consumers of it—players not makers. The creation of sound could be what was at the heart of the threat of the drum in early America, sounds not heard before, unknown rhythms. In comparison our private playing has less effect; listening has become internalized. "Can you hear the drum?" "Sorry, let me first take these earphones from my ears!" The flip side of our evolution towards personal versus group experience is that, per user, the Internet can be "heard" by more individuals than any medium ever. And, to move beyond the realm of music for a moment, we are all information makers in the digital age thanks to the ideas contained in our written and sent texts.

I am guilty of practicing what I critique here, romanticizing a cultural object about which my own knowledge is limited. I use the idea of the drum as a vehicle for an investigation of early American culture and the resistance to difference and also as a means to understand African American culture, to consider the ways in which African practices continued. Some observers captured those moments in time when both African and assimilated performances occurred: African Americans themselves speak of the drum as a past practice. I am interested in the drum as a symbol of cultural evolution, of how African Americans reclaimed the symbol of the drum by the time of the Harlem Renaissance. I have thought to create this introduction to frame my research within a broader scholarly context.

## Time and Narrative

One reference that demarcates cultural practice is time. Clock time is only one form of marking: another is the event orientation practiced in African societies. Joseph Holloway compared the American Gullah Island and African conceptions of time. He first made a distinction between circular versus linear approaches to time, the episodic and multidimensional as opposed to the abstract and linear.

This circular pattern of time is realized in such natural phenomena as birth, aging, and death: African time continues after death, because time is circular and not linear. Ancestors could be reborn back into the community of the living, or they could simply dwell in the world of ancestral spirits. For Africans, time is both sacred and profane, dividing the human world into sacred and non-sacred time, the temporal and the eternal.[18]

This explanation suggests that performance-as-event can also mark the "collective memory" of a people.[19] Furthermore, Wilfried Raussert wrote regarding the communal and sequential aspects of culture:

> Jazz, however, also experiments with a sense of time prevalent in African cultures such as Yoruba and Bantu. African cultures generally view time from a holistic perspective. Accordingly, past, present, and future exist simultaneously. . . . Time, thus remains neutral until an incident

> marks it significance. . . . The notion of an abstract temporal sequence is absent from African thinking.[20]

African Americans continued to utilize this event orientation to time. As a result, performance came to mark the day-to-day. Festive occasions brought beginnings and endings and became thresholds of progress and new thinking.

Swing in jazz, for example, is recognized as an important African American reference that is elusive to define in a temporal sense. Jürgen Grandt tracked the idea of time in African American fiction and the defining of swing by writers. That author referred to the "dynamic interaction of time and space" and presented the efforts of seven writers, critics, and musicologists to define swing.[21] All of these commentators agree that there are uniquely African American time references that punctuate music performance.

African Americans create and move to a non-Western time sense. And yet the African American experience is inexorably a part of a Western, that is, American, cultural experience. This makes the black experience a tale that can be interpreted on colonial, imperial, and postcolonial terms. Isidore Okpewho wrote regarding Derek Walcott and black writers' challenge of "the systematic appropriations of other peoples' territory and selfhood" that has been the legacy of Europe in the New World.[22] Although there may be an African and African American timeline and time sense, that discussion is framed forever within a Western construct that innately questions its value.

In addition, Ronald Rodano observed a dilemma in how black history has been presented. He wrote of "the language of white supremacy in constituting 'black music'" and asked the question "how might we engage simultaneously in black music's deconstruction and its affirmative reconstruction?"[23] Rodano found troubling the reality of African American culture's mediated story. The present study is an answer to such questions in that here I have employed the voices of African Americans themselves, along with artifacts and images, to counter the weaknesses of past bias. This version of the story complicates and creates new and various timelines in the making and telling of black music history.

The African American experience is rarely without this social tension between points of view. Clare Corbould described mid-century perspectives of the people versus the views published in newspapers in valuing the activities of the black community. One aspect of modernity is the "dissociation of sound from space through new building materials."[24] Privacy and the exclusion of noise became associated with class. In contrast, sound is also "a way to claim" a space as one's own. For blacks in Harlem "possessing the soundscape through everyday noise, as well as parades and other special occasions, they thereby lay claim to the physical space that they did not literally own and carved out their own corner of that great modern city."[25] Similarly, a discussion of time relations and narration was presented by Imani Perry, who considered the narratives in hip hop "of gangsterism, drug dealing, and other violence" and "poverty, desperation, lack of educational opportunity, or a conflicted relationship to a father."[26] Perry noted that "this expands the narrative, shifting the interpretive paradigm of outlaw activity to a sociological analysis."[27] Here the legal and the social present differing reasons behind actions. Indeed, the creation of art itself is propelled by these forces. Perry referred to the relationship of narrative content and time frame in our understanding of story.

## Thoughts and Things: Censors, Bans, and Prohibitions

When has an object, a cultural object, been banned from use by one group in order to stop the practices associated with it or simply to eliminate its use? Certainly, books have been suppressed. "Banned in Boston" is the moniker H. L. Mencken's *American Mercury* magazine wore at the time of his arrest for its unauthorized sale in 1926. Mencken's magazine admonished local Boston conservative values.[28] Seized from the shelves of bookstores for its explicit sexual content, Edmund Wilson's *Memoirs of Hecate County* was banned in 1946 in New York City. The American literary critic Lionel Trilling famously defended the artistic merits of the text in open court.[29] Among its other travails, Vladimir Nabokov's *Lolita* was prohibited in France in 1956.[30]

There are many other examples to consider. In her study of gender in Spanish religious art, Diane Apostolos-Cappadona documented how the five-finger icon of the open right hand was banned by an Episcopal Spanish junta called by Emperor Charles V in 1526. The hand functioned as a "talismanic" amulet worn by infants and women to protect the wearer from evil.[31] Scholar Michael Meyer argued that "the determination of the Jews to remain Jews seldom yielded to duress."[32] As early as 1515 there were efforts to banish Jews from the Rhine-Main areas of present day Germany and eventually from the entire Holy Roman Empire. Locally, "Jews with no visible means of support," in one instance in Haerstadt in 1740, could be banished from town.[33] There were also many restrictions for Jews in Europe in the eighteenth century. Books that were contrary to Christianity were forbidden. Copies of the Talmud, for example, were confiscated in Vienna in 1722. Rabbi David Oppenheim of Prague owned a library of seven thousand printed volumes that he arranged to have moved in 1702 to Hanover. Jewish texts were burned in Prague in 1722. Efforts at conversion and coercion to Christianity, over time, met with little success. Converts were often the physically desperate.[34]

In mid-eighteenth-century Scotland Highlander regiments were created. These army units were formed in 1757 in an effort to restore the House of Stuart with Montgomery's Highlanders and went on to multiply and carry surnames such as MacLeod, MacDonald, Argyll, Seaforth, and Gordon. "The men of the Highland regiments were the only people in Scotland, men or women, allowed to wear the tartan in any form; and their pipers were free of the eleven-year-old ban, or implied ban, on their beloved pipes."[35] Montgomery's Highlanders, by way of example, consisted of over fourteen hundred men and boasted thirty pipers and drummers. Francis Collinson contended that this context for playing the pipes "was sufficient to save the ancient art of piobaireachd from fading out and perishing of disuse."[36]

In 1917 James Joyce made the observation that "ten years of my life have been consumed in correspondence and litigation about my book *Dubliners*. It was rejected by forty publishers; three times set up, and once burnt."[37] Offensive words and phrases were the source of the book's issues with publishers. It was first published in 1914. *A Portrait of the Artist as a Young Man* was rejected by publishers and first published in the United States in 1916. Due to the censorship of the Franco regime in Spain, for example, *Portrait* was not available there until 1926.[38] Georges Van den Abbelle presented the following passage describing the reality of multiple print copies versus the single manuscript.

In the early years of the sixteenth century, not just Rabelais but the rest of his Renaissance world had come increasingly to know the heavy hand of censorship and persecution. Bookburning, of course, had lost its traditional source of terror with the invention of the printing press: no longer could a single bonfire extinguish all versions of a single manuscript. Instead, Church and State authorities had to, in the course of the Renaissance, invent new practices for controlling and regulating the circulation of dangerous words: bans on publication, excision of offensive passages prior to printing, indices of prohibited books, and so on.[39]

## The Result

At once, prohibitions have been effective and have experienced limited success. Canadians drank in spite of temperance, World War II, and a sagging economy. African Americans were susceptible to drug addiction, notably cocaine, as song lyrics from the early twentieth century attest.

*Coke, I love, coke, I buy,*
*I'm gonna sniff my coke till the day I die,*
*Hey honey, take a whiff on me.*[40]

African Americans as an oppressed and low wage-earning population were hardly the dangerous drug-consuming element that they were made out to be.

Self-censorship, whether in the Arab press or Israeli theater, is yet a response and suggests a reality of couched resistance, as is proposed by Jean Graham-Jones, in his article on theater in Argentina. It is possible that, in the mind of the artist, censors do not exist at all, as in the case of the evident success of Oscar Micheaux to distribute his films internationally. The destructive force of prohibitions is made clear by the two articles on postwar Japan. Censor as censure or condemnation of content or an artistic style is a form of violence with consequences that shape future art. Today's Kabuki is a reflection of its postwar past. The suggestion in the writing of Leo Strauss that controversy simply becomes submerged hints at the idea of surrogates or new thoughts and things to stand in the place of the old.

To return to the idea of the drum, it is arguable that the drum set, the rhythmic cornerstone of all dance band culture, was made possible by the prohibition of the African drum at an earlier time. The ban not only propelled African American culture into the evolution of hybrid forms: the ring shout, juba, the invention of the banjo, and unique performance practices on the violin (discussed later in this study). The end of the prohibition allowed for a new beginning and the creation of a musical culture that would have otherwise been remarkably different. Hence, the "djembe over the shoulder" vision with which I began.

## The Drum as Media: Rhythm and Meta Narratives

Media is a tool for communication, and the drum is one of the most primal implements of sound. Considering the drum's meta narrative, its grand or central theme, is a challenging task. What comes to my mind first is whether to base the discussion on myth or reality, Tarzan or Olatunji (with all due respect to the master drummer). I return also to the martial. Is the news good or bad, peaceful or turbulent? I admit that as an American I have been influenced by Hollywood. I do know better. Certainly, context is an important aspect of the use of drum. Possibly the answer is simply that the drum is intended for dance. Question answered. But the multitude of musical styles featuring drums are much too loaded with other aspects than to be explained solely in terms of dance. The drum brings emotion and exuberance to music. Percussion fills out, increases the volume, emphasizes moments in time, and highlights them. A driving rhythm can be political or a call for physical and emotional release. The jazz drum set, the trap set that became the drums of rock and roll and international pop then, is a true tool that has more uses than can be told. I quickly arrive at Lyotard's "incredulity" regarding the legitimacy of the idea of a global schema.[41]

Beginning in the early twentieth century, African American music's rhythms and multipurpose, for example, were new and modern. Styles arose—the blues, jazz, gospel, swing, rhythm-and-blues, and soul—and were appropriated by late century in a postmodern mode, particularly in free jazz and hip hop. The drum's role was one of catalyst. Changes in jazz rhythm marked its stylistic evolution. Bebop was fast and almost undanceable, and that was the point. Soul music borrowed widely from the sacred and the secular. For example, James Brown was as much a preacher as he was a spokesperson for the sexuality of women, and his music presented the platform for both roles. Recognized in the early 1960s, free jazz "sampled" the black music before it. Saxophonist John Coltrane, who began within the tradition and moved towards free playing, was both churchy and played faster than bop. Ornette Coleman, as well, used the simplified language of the spiritual in themes and played variations, improvizations, that were "out." Their percussionists, such as Elvin Jones and Billy Higgins, supported the experimentation and pushed these artists further than they could have gone alone. Jazz became postmodern in its discarding of previous forms, such as groups with no piano and the adoption of non-Western rhythms from Africa. Rap music's sampling is postmodern as are the music's other aspects of the feeling of personal and social fracture and the use of noise and distortion. The drum set in rap is, for the most part, a dance tool and a source of sound. African Americans make clear the many diverse roles of the drum.

Joel Dinnerstein made a case for the ways in which black culture adapted to the technological. The train-whistle guitar style of the blues becomes a coping mechanism as well as a creative interpretation of sound and the meaning of the railroad. Time and rhythm become metaphors for the Industrial Age. A German observer in 1873 saw the American railways as "great national clocks."[42] Dinnerstein noted that the wristwatch produced the first human-machine interface. Time was "manufactured" by these devices.

A favorite image of mine is that of the saxophone as an Industrial Age example of the interaction of man and device. A brass instrument, pressed and pounded into a curving form, with some horns appearing almost as tall as their players, the saxophone's sound is an extension of the human voice. By way of metal and reed the performer becomes post-human. The sensual form of the instrument, the baritone saxophone curves up and over itself, is, almost as a contradiction, covered with keys. With keys of all sizes with apparently complex systems of rods, springs, and buttons, the instrument presents a mechanical-sexual profile. The sound is unmistakable. It is ironic that this instrument, created by the Belgian Adolph Sax, who sought a hybrid between woodwind and brass, was rejected in Western Europe as a symphonic instrument and first given a special voice by black men. The horn's sound belies its materials and complexity. Over time, what began as a take on the human voice evolved into a reflection of the industrial era. Saxophone playing became more harmonic and less melodic, and the improvization quickened. The horn started to sound like the city. To play a major sixth in the right way can imitate an early automobile horn. Players vary in how they appear while playing the instrument in jazz. Some appear to be locked in struggle with an adversary, others hold the instrument like a significant other. Dinnerstein's discussion suggests that Industrial Age technology itself was a carrier of a message. Neither drum nor horn so much carry a specific rhythm or beat but act as a harbinger, a catalyst. African Americans paid homage to technology and change—and Charles Lindbergh—by naming a dance the Lindy Hop, for example. That author concluded that this way of articulating a relationship with American technology has been and continues to be a useful tool.

Alexander Weheliye critiqued more than what he calls the "postdiscipline" of cultural studies. He pointed to the virtual whiteness of cyber theory, how "the erasure of race severely limits how we conceive of the complex interplay between 'humans' and informational technologies." His piece presents the story of the "vocoder, a speech-synthesizing device that renders the human voice robotic." The focus is placed on a kind of sonic subjectivity as opposed to the ocular, its production and reception. The word "feenin,'" referring to having a love addiction and being a fiend, was used by the group Jodeci in 1993. The group used synthesized voices in the recording. Weheliye described how rap music lyrics have included the technological consumer items of their time and have previously featured the cell phone, in Missy Elliott's "Beep Me 911," and the pager, in Destiny's Child's "Bug-a-Boo." The black voice is a charged symbol. There is a contradiction in the enhanced status of the performer, the celebrity, the voice, and the reality of the artist's body as a person, not as a commodity. The voices of Stevie Wonder or Aretha Franklin have much more meaning to us than their visuality, over time. How these artists looked over the years does not have the same importance as the way that their voices embody them. The voice is larger than life in spite of the fact that the black body of the artist is a potential site of bias in a racist society.[43]

Michael Chaney emphasized the African American and technological links made by Ishmael Reed in *Flight to Canada* (1976). In an interview, Reed described the "cyborgization" of African Americans in the form of tokenism. When an individual becomes a celebrity, he or she is transformed by the media into a manufactured "pawn." It is the transmission and control of the image of the individual that makes for this state. Chaney found that in Reed's fiction the relationship between technology and race possesses rules of assimilation and exclusion. Outsiders mime, and, as in minstrelsy, imitate the imitators. The black persona is subjected to a demoralizing control.[44] Ronald Radano's "Soul Texts and the Blackness of Folk" (1995) is an analysis of an evolution from folk to media form for the African American spiritual. The focus is the trope of double consciousness as famously deployed by W. E. B. Du Bois and the tale of the Fisk Jubilee Singers and their reinvention as concert artists for the international stage in the late nineteenth century. The Jubilee Singers provided a presentation of the spiritual, a folk form that was packaged into a medium, an implement, one that came to symbolize black America. Radano viewed the ideas of Du Bois and others on the meaning of the Singers. What is relevant here is the appropriation by whites and African Americans of black cultural roots. Paul Gilroy wrote about the Jubilee Singers in *The Black Atlantic* (1993) and argued that the group was made media-ready via tours in America and then England. Furthermore, Radano contended that "because the idea of an authentic African American music performed by blacks themselves arose during a historical period still dominated by minstrel parody, that 'realness' could be little more than a fiction once the spirituals emerged as a national concept."[45]

This discussion points to the reality that American culture had a way of fixing a version of African American artistic expression. Whether token, pawn, or folk, mainstream culture distills art and at the same time stereotypes it. African American expression in particular as a kind of outsider art is ripe for bias as the creators have been over time an American antithesis. I will argue, based on the material in the larger study, that white Americans prior to the twentieth century rarely saw true black performance, as it was to a great extent a clandestine activity. As European travelers who arrive in the Americas make clear, they were dumbfounded by the dancing and drumming they witnessed, and they either degraded it as the devil's work or stumbled over themselves to conjure an accurate picture of what they saw and heard.

The idea of African American influence, of black expression, of black music as an agent of change, of the notion of black rhythm as spark or an ignition, all come to a point in the early twentieth century. In a consideration of media, the black experience, and change, Pamela Caughie in "Passing as Modernism" (2005) viewed the relationship between identity and technology after the turn of the last century. She observed that

> through the swift dissemination of cultural products (e.g., music, literature, fashion) worldwide by means of new technologies and the forces of mass culture, the borders separating nations and geographic regions, like those separating races and genders, became permeable and insecure.[46]

The Industrial Age challenged identity and also pushed the populace to try out difference via commodity markets. In her view, African American culture became synonymous with the new communication and broadcasting technologies. What she calls "border crossing" involved whites becoming an other to enact the new ways of the jazz era. For Caughie, "the New Negro craze fueled by the popularity of jazz was propelled across the Atlantic by the talking machine, the wireless, and the cinema."[47] The beginning of the twentieth century saw the creation of a link between culture and media as they became interdependent. The instrument, the technology, was the carrier of identity in a commercial form to be chosen and purchased.

## The Body

How is the body like a drum? What is the relationship between the black slave's body and the tools that the slave employed? Certainly, the black body has been an important subject of discussion in postcolonial studies. Maggie Montesinos Sale described the 1839 Amistad affair regarding the slaves who commandeered a ship in the Caribbean from where it eventually sailed to the northeast coast of America. The ship was captured, and the trial brought into public view the African crewmember Joseph Cinque, who became a heroic figure, a "hyper-African" in the words of the author.[48] His dream was to return home to Africa; his tool was a ship. Ships are masculine spaces themselves, the author reminds us, although the vessel itself is "manned," and it is "she" who carries the crew. Lisa Collins surveyed the visualization of black women—from Edouard Manet's "Olympia" (1865), the famous painting of a young reclining nude woman that depicts a black maid, to African American artist Renée Stout's "Fetish #2" (1988), which is a cast of her own nude body. Collins claimed that "every female slave narrative includes a reference to rape."[49] Black bodies in the Americas have been objects of bondage and violence. Bodies themselves have been used as tools. Jody Blake documented that performer Josephine Baker became a "black idol" in France.[50] Jazz and Modernism's "stylistic barbarism" garnered a negative reaction on the Continent as the Charleston dance was linked to "social delinquency" and as there was a call to ban certain dance steps of an "exotic" nature. Here the body becomes a symbol: the black body is a site of sensuality that disseminates a moral message through movement. The black body acts as a medium, a means of transmission, a conduit, or pathway.

## The Image of Sound

In *How Early America Sounded* (2005), Richard Cullen Rath presented African drumming in the New World as largely a threat to be controlled. Europeans saw the drumming of Africans as "powerful tools of state." In a section on the Stono Rebellion, the author acknowledged a reversal of the "Hegelian master/slave dialectic" as slave owners feared the potential of their bondsmen. He found that masters "understood only the soundways of military state drumming that they shared with Africans." Planters, in fact, "misapprehended" the "instrumental soundways" of African Americans. My work seeks to answer this very point. Europeans mythologized the meaning of the drum. Yes, there was a martial drum, but that was only one of a pantheon of uses for the instrument. Otherwise we miss the African American application of their rhythmic heritage.[51] In *The Sounds of Slavery* (2006), Graham White and coauthor presented few drum examples. This is in contrast to Rath's piece, which documented many examples by travel writers, such as Sir Hans Sloane, whose material will appear later here. In fact, there are but four instances in the entire text of *Sounds*, one of which, the account of surveyor Benjamin Latrobe, will be covered here as well in a later chapter. *Sounds* does cover the African American vocal traditions using early American observers as a resource for the presentations of religious song and the ring shout.[52]

The rhythmic heritage of the African diaspora was central to the practice of capoeira in Brazil during the nineteenth century. Maya Chvaicer described how this competitive martial arts dance form was initially viewed as play, a game. The sport became disruptive in the locales where it was practiced. The author pointed out that, because the game was played by African slaves, whites further labeled the activity as savage. In 1831 a decree sought the arrest of participants in capoeira. This period also saw an increase in the slave population so these legal measures may have been in part an inevitable consequence. By mid-century the name became associated with crime and gangs. Most Africans arriving in Rio de Janeiro in the first decade of the nineteenth century came from west central Africa, suggesting an important link for the origin of capoeira. This designated criminal element became ethnically diverse in Brazil, possibly in coincidence with the end of the Atlantic slave trade in 1850. Police records show that "capoeiras" took on whites in their ranks by mid century. It was not until after Brazil's late century conflict with Paraguay, where many capoeiras fought, that the form became associated with martial arts. The author continued, with the following explanation that connects the practice with other social realms.

For the African slaves in the early 1800s, capoeira was, therefore, a social expression that inherently incorporated all the basic elements of an African game: the circle, dance, music, audience, as well as the rituals and symbols that served capoeiras in the course of this activity; it contained all the supplementary Congolese ingredients of a game to train and prepare the individual for his daily life. As a process that mirrored life itself, it provided the player with the required experience to strengthen the body and the soul. As any other African activity, it contained elements that combined the sacred with the secular; in other words, both gods and the dead were active participants in the event.

This complexity is a broad contrast from the narrower view of capoeira as simply a martial practice. Europeans misread the nature of the game and saw only its threatening aspects.[53]

Furthermore, observation has been shown to be susceptible to bias that is both cultural, practice-based, and racial in relation to identity. Mark Smith made points regarding the cultural conventions of our olfactory consciousness, for example, describing the scholarship of Charles Hoffer, regarding "the mediated and conflicted nature of sensory encounters between Europeans and Native Americans" as well as "the aurality and visuality of the 1739 South Carolina Stono slave rebellion." The need to control the unknown is ripe with bias. Describing the work of Alain Corbin on the rural French in the nineteenth century, "the sounds of bells to particular groups held an emotional meaning that went deeper than even music and could illicit reactions that would be largely unintelligible to—and hidden from—a wholly visualist history."[54]

For the colonial era African diaspora, by way of example there is a watercolor by Jean Baptist Debret titled "Le Viel Orphée Africain Oricongo" that is plate 38 in Viagem pitoresca e histórica ao Brasil from 1834.[55] Pictured is a group of African slaves in Brazil: in the center of the image is an elderly man who appears blind. "Old Orpheus" plays the oricongo, today known as the berimbau (see Illustration 0.1). This instrument, which is still in use today, is associated with capoeira. He is being led by the boy in the image, as the musician is a begger. This man, most likely an Angolan, is a musician and vocalist, as one variant of the image is titled "The Blind Singer," and Debret writes "the performer's aptitude for music is immediately apparent." In "Le Viel Orphée Africain Oricongo," the artist shows an attentive group of women and one child surrounding the performer. One woman on the right, and possibly a woman on the left, appear to call out to the old man.

*Illustration 0.1* "Le Viel Orphée Africain Oricongo." Jean Baptist Debret. 1834.

Source: Plate 38 in *Viagem pitoresca e histórica ao Brasil*. 1834. Enciclopédia Itaú Cultural de Arte e Cultura Brasileiras. São Paulo.

What can this "visualist" display tell us about the aural world of the African in early eighteenth-century Brazil? Debret used the image of the man and boy in at least two works. The group image in color is dated 1826 in the lower left corner; another image, of the man and boy and another musician on a lamellophone (thumb piano) appeared in a published text of 1834.

The group scene suggests that the berimbau was played in many contexts and not only accompanied capoeira. This man is also singing with a group of women as an audience. This is not a male domain. By this context the artist portrays a multifaceted aspect to performance and social display that could include for this man the definitions of troubador, begger, or skilled musician and masterful vocalist.[56]

Two contemporary examples of interpretation and the monitoring of meaning in African American performance are "Black Faces, White Voices: The Politics of Dubbing in *Carmen Jones*" (2003) by Jeff Smith and "All That You Can't Leave Behind: Black Female Soul Singing and the Politics of Surrogation in the Age of Catastrophe" (2008) by Daphne Brooks. Both are essays devoted to the African American female voice and the political implications of black women's performances. Smith considered the myriad of circumstances that brought about the dubbing of the 1954 film *Carmen Jones* starring Dorothy Dandridge. This musical, with lyrics by Oscar Hammerstein and directed by Otto Preminger, featured an all-black cast starring Harry Belafonte, Pearl Bailey, and Diahann Carroll, among others. Professional operatic vocalists were hired to dub the songs of Dandridge, Belafonte, and Carroll, but not Bailey. The author cited the navigation of intentions for the film's producers.

This sense of a cultural hierarchy is further reinforced by two complementary hierarchies within the film. The first of these is evident in the film's treatment of the division of speech and song. While a crude approximation of vernacular language is evident within the film's dialogue and song lyrics, this example of folk culture is juxtaposed with the melodies, harmonies, and orchestration of Western classical music. It is within this split between speech and song that the latter becomes a repository of the values of high culture and "whiteness," while the former retains the broader associations with spontaneity, naturalness, and folk expression.[57]

Here blackness is deemed too much a force for the American film audience. Billy Rose's production of the show first played in Philadelphia in 1943. The Hollywood version, with the assistance of dubbing technology, created the surreal illusion of black actors with white singing voices. Marilyn Horne, who sang Dandridge's parts, sang "smearing" her tone, as an adopted affectation. Thus, white singers sing black for black actors who's singing is too black. The argument can be made that the demands of Bizet's piece was the issue, but Rose's show had been around for a decade up to the film's creation. Other African Americans obviously sang it.

This example is about more than simply the control of black sound. Smith presents the conundrum as a form of minstrelsy. In a sense the African American cast are mechanized by this arrangement of instant operatic voices, turned into automatons. I have, in fact, marveled at the vocal ensembles in particular, they sounded so proper, before I knew about the dubbing. The example of *Carmen Jones* represents a form of sonic surveillance, not a ban but a withdrawal, a silencing of the true nature and abilities, of the African American cast. In "Black Faces" Brooks profiles African American female vocalists Mary J. Blige and Beyoncé Knowles for how their persona represents a continuum of dissonance and resistance. Blige and Knowles are self-made in the sense that they are a success because of the broad range that their art has addressed. Under the heading of dissonance I would add to Brooks's list Dinah Washington, Eartha Kitt, and Patti LaBelle as artists spanning different generations whose persona challenged existing norms. The author's narrative made the chilling point that the person of contemporary African American professionals has come under attack, via harassment and "media scrutiny," in spite of their professional success. Dissonance, for Brooks, is met with a systemic response as conventions are challenged. For example, Beyoncé's "Ring the Alarm" features a dramatization of her being arrested. This is both "sonic" protest and "hypervisibility."[58]

## Notes

1 See, for example, John Blassingame, *The Slave Community: Plantation Life in the Antebellum South* (New York: Oxford University Press, 1972), 41.
2 This language is taken from the South Carolina Slave Act of 1740. See *The Statutes at Large of South Carolina: Acts Relating to Charleston, Courts, Slaves, and Rivers*, Vol. 7, ed. David J. McCord (Columbia, SC: A. S. Johnston, 1840).
3 For the direct words of African Americans for my research I reviewed interviews from The Federal Writers' Project, *The American Slave: A Composite Autobiography*, 22 vols., ed. George P. Rawick (Westport, CT: Greenwood Press, 1972–1979), and The Georgia Writers' Project, *Savannah Unit, Work Projects Administration, Drums and Shadows: Survival Studies among the Georgia Coastal Negroes* (Athens: University of Georgia Press, 1986). Both are subsets of the Slave Narrative Collection held by the Library of Congress, which includes 2,000 interviews and text totaling 10,000 typed pages, photographs, and recordings. Rawick's efforts in the 1970s pulled together interviews from Mississippi and other Southern states that were never part of the Library of Congress collection. *Drums and Shadows* contains interviews specific to the Georgia Sea Islands. The present study concentrates on this collection.
4 Lynne Emery, *Black Dance in the United States from 1615 to 1970* (Princeton: Princeton University Press, 1972).
5 Dena J. Epstein, *Sinful Tunes and Spirituals: Black Folk Music to the Civil War* (Chicago: University of Chicago Press, 1977).
6 *Readings in Black American Music*, ed. Eileen Southern (New York: W. W. Norton, 1971), and Eileen Southern, *African American Traditions in Song, Sermon Tale, and Dance, 1600s–1920* (Westport, CT: Greenwood, 1990).
7 John F. Szwed and Roger D. Abrahams, *Afro-American Folk Culture: An Annotated Bibliography of Materials from North, Central, and South America and the West Indies* (Philadelphia: Institute for the Study of Human Issues, 1978).
8 John Szwed mentions the coincidence of drum citations over time in his Afro-American Folk Culture.
9 Writers' Program. Georgia. *Drums and Shadows; Survival Studies among the Georgia Coastal Negroes* (Savannah Unit, Georgia Writers' Project, Work Projects Administration. Athens. 1940).
10 Sterling Stuckey, *Going through the Storm: The Influence of African American Art in History* (New York: Oxford University Press, 1993), 3–6.
11 See Mary Ryan, *Cradle of the Middle Class* (New York: Cambridge University Press, 1983), and Patricia Nelson Limerick, *The Legacy of Conquest* (New York: W. W. Norton, 1987).
12 See Baby Dodds and Larry Gara, *The Baby Dodds Story* (Los Angeles: Contemporary Press, 1959) for a narrative of the creation, standardization, and market-

ing of the trap set. Baby Dodds was a New Orleans drummer whose brother was the jazz clarinetist Johnny Dodds.

13 See John Michael Vlach, *The Afro-American Tradition in Decorative Arts* (Cleveland: Cleve-Land Museum of Art, 1978) for examples that include architecture, boat building and iron work.
14 David Nye, *Consuming Power: A Social History of American Energies* (Cambridge: MIT Press, 1999), 163.
15 See Robert Johnson, *The Complete Recordings* (Columbia Records, 1990).
16 Benjamin Henry Boneval Latrobe, *Impressions Respecting New Orleans: Diary & Sketches, 1818–1820* (New York: Columbia University Press, 1951), 49–51.
17 Ralph Ellison, *Invisible Man* (New York: Randon House, 1952), 7–8. "Now I have one radio-phonograph; I plan to have five."
18 Joseph Holloway, "Time in the African Diaspora: The Gullah Experience," in *Time in the Black Experience*, ed. Joseph K. Adjaye (Westport, CT: Greenwood Press, 1994), 93–4.
19 Ibid. 200–2.
20 William Raussert, *Negotiating Temporal Differences: Blues, Jazz and Narrativity in African American Culture* (Heidelberg: C. Winter, 2000), 4.
21 Jürgen Grandt, *Kinds of Blue: The Jazz Aesthetic in African American Narrative* (Columbus, OH: Ohio State Press), 31.
22 Isidore Okpewho, "Walcott, Homer, and the 'Black Atlantic'," *Research in African Literature* 33/1 (Spring 2002), 27–44.
23 Ronald Rodano, "Narrating Black Music's Past," *Radical History Review* 84 (2002), 115–18.
24 Clare Corbould, "Streets, Sounds and Identity in Interwar Harlem," *Journal of Social History* 40 (Summer 2007), 861.
25 Ibid. 861.
26 Imani Perry, *Prophets of the Hood* (Durham: Duke University Press, 2004), 108.
27 Ibid.
28 Herbert N. Foerstel, *Banned in the Media: A Reference Guide to Censorship in the Press* (Westport, CT: Greenwood Press, 1998), 63.
29 Louis Menard, "Introduction to Edmund White, Memoirs of Hecate County," *New York Review of Books* (2004), xi.
30 Brian Boyd, *Vladimir Nabokov: The American Years* (Princeton: Princeton University Press, 1993), 357.
31 Diane Apostolos-Cappadona, "Discerning the Hand of Fatima: An Iconological Investigation of the Role of Gender in Religious Art," in *Beyond the Exotic: Women's Histories in Islamic Societies*, ed. Amira El-Azhary Sonbol (Syracuse: Syracuse University Press, 2005), 357.
32 Michael A. Meyer, *Tradition and Enlightenment, 1600–1780, Vol. I of German-Jewish History in Modern Times* (New York: Columbia University Press, 1996), 61, 246, and 160.
33 Ibid. 246.
34 Ibid. 160.
35 Francis Collinson, *The Bagpipe* (London: Routledge & Kegan Paul, 1975), 174–5.
36 Ibid.
37 James Joyce, quoted in Albert Lazaro, "James Joyce's Encounters with Spanish Censorship, 1939–1966," *Joyce Studies Annual* 12 (2001), 38–40.
38 Ibid. 38–39.
39 Georges Van den Abbelle, "The Persecution of Writing: Revisiting Strauss and

Censorship," *Diacritics* 27/2 (1997), 3.

40 Michael Cohen, "Jim Crow's Drug War: Race, Coca Cola, and the Southern Origins of Drugs," *Southern Cultures* 12/3 (Fall 2006), 71.

41 Jean-Francois Lyotard, "Simplifying to the Extreme, I Define Postmodern as Incredulity toward Metanarratives," *The Postmodern Condition* (1979), xxiv–xxv.

42 Joel Dinnerstein, *Swinging the Machine: Modernity, Technology, and African American Culture* (Amherst: University of Massachusetts Press, 2003), 39.

43 Alexander Weheliye, "'Feenin': Posthuman Voices in Contemporary Black Popular Music," *Social Text* 20/2 (2002), 21–47.

44 Michael Chaney, "Slave Cyborgs and the Black Infovirus: Ishmael Reed's Cybernetic Aesthetics," *Modern Fiction Studies* 49/2 (2003), 261–83.

45 Ronald Radano, "Soul Texts and the Blackness of Folk," *Modernism/Modernity* 2/1 (1995), 71–95. Paul Gilroy, *The Black Atlantic* (Cambridge, MA: Harvard University Press 1993).

46 Pamela Caughie, "Passing as Modernism," *Modernism/Modernity* 12/3 (2005), 385–406.

47 Ibid.

48 Maggie Montesinos Sale, *The Slumbering Volcano: American Slave Ship Revolts and the Production of Violent Masculinities* (City: Publisher, 1997).

49 Lisa Collins, "Economies of Flesh: Representing the Black Female Body in Art," in *Skin Deep, Spirit Strong: The Black Female Body in American Culture*, ed. Kimberly Gisele Wallace-Sanders (Ann Arbor: University of Michigan Press, 2002).

50 Jody Blake, *Le Tumulte Noir: Modernist Art and Popular Entertainment in Jazz-Age Paris, 1900–1930* (University Park, PA: Penn State University Press, 1999).

51 Richard Cullen Rath, *How Early America Sounded* (Ithaca: Cornell University Press, 2005), 79, 89.

52 Graham White, *The Sounds of Slavery* (Boston: Beacon Press, 2006).

53 Maya Chvaicer, "The Criminalization of Capoeira in Nineteenth century Brazil," *Hispanic American Historical Review* 82/3 (2002), 525–47. See Walter Rucker, *The River Flows on: Black Resistance, Culture, and Identity Formation in Early America* (Baton Rouge: Louisiana State University Press, 2006), 104–9, for examples of game and competitive dance with rhythmic accompaniment in West Central Africa, Brazil, and South Carolina. See Lois Wilcken, *Encyclopedia of Slave Resistance and Rebellion*, ed. Junius Rodriguez (2007), 337–9. She provided a thorough summary of African American music during slavery with a mention of capoeira and the idea of surrogate use.

54 Mark Smith, "Producing Sense, Consuming Sense, Making Sense: Perils and Prospects for Sensory History," *Journal of Social History* 40/4 (2007), 841–58. In James Billington, "Bell and Canon," in *The Icon and the Axe: An Interpretive History of Russian Culture* (New York: Vintage, 1970), 37–8, the author described how the bell was a "media" used with great "intensity and imagination" in fifteenth century Kiev. He referred to an "interaction of sight and sound" that became important aspects of the deeply religious culture that was developing at the time.

55 Jean Baptist Debret, *Viagem Pitoresca e Histórica ao Brasil* (Paris: Firmin-Dido Fréres, 1834).

56 Peter Fryer, *Rhythms of Resistance: African Musical Heritage in Brazil* (London: Pluto Press, 2000), 35.

57 Jeff Smith, "Black Faces, White Voices: The Politics of Dubbing in Carmen Jones," *The Velvet Light Trap* 51 (2003), 29–42, 38.
58 Daphne Brooks, "'All That You Can't Leave Behind': Black Female Soul Singing and the Politics of Surrogation in the Age of Catastrophe," *Meridians: Feminism, Race, Transnationalism* 8/1 (2008), 180–204.

# 1 Observers of Culture

Who cares about African culture in America? Who cared about Africans in America? In answer to the second question, enough people created a system of chattel slavery for which Africans were the choice. In reply to the first, numerous people observed and recorded African culture in the Americas as something foreign and often inexplicable. Tour descriptions, journal entries, and vignettes in articles about the South often looked to reflect on what America was becoming, or had become and used the observation of black culture sometimes as a gauge to portray the ways of this land. Slave narratives and the interviews of former slaves are distant and not always approving reflections on a less acculturated past. Regardless of judgment, many reflected on the African ways of American slaves.

The descriptions presented here focus not on African American culture but on African culture in America: that is, the handmade drum, played by hands or sticks and used as music for dance, communication, weddings, funerals, harvest celebrations, Christmas, and other fetes. To open this study of the drum in the Americas, this chapter will focus on those who saw and wrote the accounts.

## Founding Fathers and Literary Giants

To make the case that the drum and African culture in general was noticed and discussed in early America, one need only to survey the prominent individuals, some well known in their own time and some more popular in ours, who have remarked on the use of the drum, the African-like rhythmic practices of the slave, or black musical abilities in general. Benjamin Franklin, while in London in 1774, talked about the situation of the free black in America in a letter, dated 20 March, to the Marquis de Condorcet. He ended his discussion with the comment that "They make good Musicians."[1] Thomas Jefferson, craftsman of the Constitution, slaveholder, and lover to black mistress Sally Hemmings, commented on African-styled music in his 1781 piece, "Notes on the State of Virginia": "The instrument proper to them is the Banjan, which they brought hither from Africa, and which is the original of the guitar, its chords being precisely the four lower chords of the guitar."[2]

J. Hector St. John de Crevecoeur's *Letters from an American Farmer* of 1782 is known for the use of language that portrays the lifestyle of the American yeoman as an exercise in a type of noble independence. De Crevecoeur is often quoted in American historical writing and has given credence to the Jeffersonian concept of a nation built on a population of autonomous agrarians. De Crevecoeur relates his experiences in Orange County, New York, mentions the "Negro fiddle," the celebrations blacks shared with their masters and the fact that they had "their own meetings."[3]

Benjamin Rush, a doctor and friend of Benjamin Franklin, had some concern for the American slave, and his 1788 "Diseases Peculiar to the Negroes" considers the role of culture for the slave.

> We are told by their masters, they are the happiest people in the world. . . . Instead of considering the songs and dances . . . as marks of their happiness, I have long considered them as physical symptoms of Melancholy Madness, and therefore as certain of their misery.[4]

Rush's statement, at once insightful and incredible, suggests the distance and lack of intimacy such observations have with the reality of the slave.

In 1805 John Pierpont of Litchfield, Connecticut, observed in his journal the slaves of Georgetown District, South Carolina, where he had taken up a position as tutor at Colonel William Allston's Monjetta Plantation.

> [in] the state of South Carolina, Christmas is a holiday, together with 2 of the succeeding days . . . for the negroes. . . . On my first waking, the sound of serenading violins and drums saluted my ears, and for some time continued. . . . During almost the whole of the second and 3rd afternoons . . . was crowded with these [?] dancers . . . fiddlers and drumming. . . . Some of them who were native Africans did not join the dance with the others, but, by themselves gave us a specimen of the sports and amusement with which the benighted and uncivilized children of nature divert themselves.[5]

Here Pierpont described fiddlers and drums, pointed out those slaves who were assimilated as opposed to those who were not and made clear the African nature of the "sport."

The architect Benjamin Latrobe, "surveyor of the public buildings" under Thomas Jefferson and civil engineer, has left in his papers descriptions and drawings from his experiences in New Orleans. In 1819, possibly while involved with his plans for a waterworks for New Orleans, Latrobe recorded his impressions of performances that he saw in Congo Square. His accounts, which are among the longest and most detailed, will be considered in Chapter Two.

English author Charles Dickens visited New York in 1842 and recounted in his American Notes a performance by "Master Juba," William Henry Lane, the African American dancer:

> suddenly the lively hero dashes in to the rescue. Instantly the fiddler grins, and goes at it tooth and nail; there is new energy in the tambourine. . . . Single shuffle, double shuffle, cut and crosscut: snapping his fingers, rolling his eyes, turning his knees, presenting the backs of his legs in front, spinning about on his toes and heels like nothing but the man's fingers on the tambourine; dancing with two left legs, two right legs, two wooden legs, two wire legs, two spring legs—all sorts of legs and no legs—what is this to him?[6]

Frederick Law Olmsted, landscape architect, is best known for his design for Central Park in New York City. He also designed the grounds surrounding the Capitol in Washington, D.C., and Mount Royal Park in Montreal. Early in his career and as a result of his antislavery beliefs, he was sent by *The New York Times* to report on the conditions of slavery in the South. His *A Journey in the Seaboard Slave States, with Remarks on Their Economy* of 1859 described plantation funerals and juba dancing.[7]

American authors Mark Twain and Charles Dudley Warner in their 1873 book *The Gilded Age: A Tale of Today* also described dance. Their book, which named this age of the post–Civil War era and took the form of a financial and political satire, made mention of two small boys "breaking down a juba in approved style."[8]

Later in the century another Englishman, Rudyard Kipling, witnessed a black church service during his visit to America in 1899. He described participants in the service dancing up the aisle and compared the dance to a "Zanzibar stick dance."[9] Finally among this group of individuals of note are archaeologist Charles Peabody's observations in his 1903 article "Notes on Negro Music" that appeared in the *Journal of American Folklore*. His comments on folk music also mentioned "rhythmic matters."[10]

## Planters

In their unique position as slaveholders, planters described their interests in and concerns for the pastimes of their slaves. Le Page du Pratz, a Louisiana plantation owner whose impressions will be described in more detail in Chapter Three, expressed his fears of the possibility of revolt in his 1758 *Histoire de la Louisianne*, regarding the large assemblies of blacks that met on Sundays under what he described as a pretext to dance.[11] Matthew Lewis provided commentary in his *Journal of a West India Proprietor* on a holiday given to his slaves in 1816 in Cornwall, Jamaica, where the musical instruments were only African.

> The music consisted of nothing by Gambys (Eboe drums), Shaky-shekies, and Kitty-katties; the latter is nothing but any flat piece of board beat upon with two sticks, and the former is a bladder with a parcel of pebbles in it. But the principal part of the music to which they dance is vocal.[12]

Another planter, Marly, from Jamaica, described in a work published in 1828 the use of the drum in an end of the sugar making season celebration known as "crop over."

> Immediately . . . the negroes assembled in and around the boiling house, dancing and rearing for joy, to the sound [of] the gumba. . . . This favorite instrument of music, the gumba, consists of a square box, with a piece of sheep's skin on each end, and though only beat with a single stick, and incapable of marking any tune, yet the negroes seemed delighted with it, and danced in the true African Fashions . . . at the same time, singing as loud as their lungs would permit.[13]

The gumba is also described in use at Christmas time.

> field negroes from the country flocked into the town . . . severally accompanied with their favorite gumba and a Fife. Though the sound of the gumba is any thing but pleasant, the principal actors drew numbers of spectators around it.

Englishman John Riland left an account that includes the use of a drum from a slave ship on which he traveled.

> The captain again wanted the slaves to dance; but they did not seem disposed to comply with his wish. . . . Sometimes a drum was carried on the main-deck, to the music of which the men sung and danced.[14]

In *A Woman Rice Planter*, Patience Pennington described Christmas festivities and dancing with music provided by slaves playing the fiddle, tambourine, bones, the drum, and sticks.[15]

Of this group of proprietors there is a range of interests and concerns about African music, dance, and drumming. Most of them simply described performance in the context of celebration or some other function. As a group there are no examples of the drum specifically in use for communication for slave revolts. This issue will also be examined at greater length in Chapter Three.

## Doctors[16]

One physician's account has already been presented here in the words of Dr. Benjamin Rush, but observations from others occur in the literature. Alexander Falconbridge served as a surgeon on slave ships from 1780 to 1787 and left the following observation:

> Exercise being deemed necessary for the preservation of their health, they are sometimes obliged to dance. . . . Their musick, upon these occasions, consists of a drum, sometimes with only one head; and when that is worn out, they do not scruple to make use of the bottom of one of the tubs.[17]

This account is, of course, similar to that of John Riland's.

Dr. John Wyeth, also a planter, wrote of the rhythmic accompaniment known as "juba" among the slaves on his plantation in the mid-nineteenth century. The drum was for the most part not available to slaves in America, so "patting juba" could be considered an alternative to the drum. Juba will be considered later in this study, but Wyeth made another comment useful to the present discussion: "The real negro music as I knew it was, as one would expect, simple and crude, and quite unlike that which modern negro minstrelsy has made popular."[18] Although Dr. Wyeth does not call the slave music African, he does distinguish African American performance from its minstrel equivalent.

Sometime before 1811, when slavery still existed in New York State and when he was a youth, Dr. James Eights witnessed Pinkster Day, a Pentecost Sunday celebration observed by slaves mostly in the North:

> The dance had its peculiarities, as well as everything else connected with this august celebration. . . . The music made use of on this occasion, was likewise singular in the extreme. The principal instrument selected to furnish this important portion of the ceremony was a symmetrically formed wooden article usually denominated [by] an eel-pot, with a cleanly dressed sheep skin drawn tightly over its wide and open extremity.[19]

An African known as King Charley, who drummed and led the dancing, was described by Eights as "tall, thin, and athletic; and although the frost of nearly seventy winters had settled on his brow, its chilling influence had not yet extended to his bosom."

## Travelers—French Monks and Slave Dealers

Travelers presented by far the most voluminous accounts of African and African American music and dance. From as early as 1620, individuals on tour in Africa and the Americas, notably aristocrats and military personnel, recorded impressions of what they saw and heard. This is the most diverse group of those providing accounts. A few of these described in telling detail African instrumental performance practices.

Richard Jobson traveled in Africa from 1620 to 1621 and recorded in the greatest detail a number of African instruments. He described the West African balafon, a xylophone-like instrument that he called the "balafo." William Smith placed an illustration of the "balafoe" [sic] as the frontispiece to his A New Voyage to Guinea of 1744.[20]

> They have little varietie of instruments, that which is most common in use, is made of a great gourd, and a necke thereunto fastned, resembling, in some sort, our Bandora; but they have no manner of fret, and the strings they are either such as the place yeeldes, or their invention can attaine to make, being very unapt to yeeld a sweete and musicall sound, notwithstanding with pinnes they winde and bring to agree in tunable notes, having not above sixe strings upon their greatest instrument: In consortship with this they have many times another who playes upon a little drumme which he holds under his left arme, and with a crooked sticke in his right hand, and his naked fingers on the left he strikes the drumme.[21]

This account mentions a type of stringed instrument with a gourd body and unfretted neck. Similar descriptions from the Americas reoccur later in this study. This African portrayal can serve as a basis for comparison. Jobson also described a small drum, held under the arm and played with a curved wooden stick. This is the talking drum or friction drum well known in West African countries.

French monk Jean Baptist Labat traveled to the island of Martinique in 1694 as a missionary. He described the dance, "la calenda," and drums.

> two drums made from the tree trunks of unequal length, each with an open end and one covered with skinlike parchment. The larger, called

> "le guard tambour," was three or four feet long and fifteen or sixteen inches in diameter. The smaller, called the "baboula," was about the same length, but eight or nine inches in diameter. The drummers held them between their legs and played them with the four fingers of both hands. The larger provided the basic beat, while the smaller was played as fast as possible.[22]

In Virginia in 1784 John Smyth reported on the use of a "banjor," which is described as a large hollow instrument with three strings, and a drum-like instrument called a "qua-qua."[23] The slave trader Nicholas Owen, while on a trip to the west coast of Africa sometime after 1746, described music: "Their chief diversions is playing upon a certain instrument of wood which sounds like a bad fiddle; this instrument is called a BANGELO; they have likewise drums and other games."[24] William Beckford provided names for the rhythm instruments of slaves, describing a "gomba, which they strike with their hands," and a "cotter, upon which they beat with sticks" during his visit to Jamaica in 1790.[25] Bryan Edwards mentioned two different drums during his travels in the Caribbean.

> The Dundo is precisely a tabor; and the Gombay is a rustic drum; being formed of the trunk of a hollow tree, one end of which is covered with a sheep's skin. From such instruments nothing like a regular tune can be expected, nor is it attempted.[26]

It is interesting to note the observation that no "tune" could be played on the drum. Marly's description from 1828 also points out that the drum was "incapable of marking any tune." Pitch variations are an element of African drumming. Possibly to the European ear a performance without melody in a traditional sense could not be considered music at all.

Baron von Sack experienced New Year's celebrations in Surinam in 1806 and remembered drumming among blacks: "The musical instruments are chiefly pieces of hollow trees, the upper part covered with leather like a drum, and are beaten with sticks."[27] Cynric Williams describes African-like practices during his visit to Jamaica in 1823.

> they again assembled on the lawn before the house with their gombays, bonjans, and an ebo drum. . . . Some of the women carried small calabashes with pebbles in them, stuck on short sticks, which they rattled in time to the songs. . . . They divided themselves into parties to dance, some before the gombays, in a ring. . . . Others performed . . . before the ebo drummer. . . . On all these occasions of festivity the mulattos kept aloof . . . and some . . . objected to participate in the heathen practices of

> their ancestors. . . . I was a little quizzed for remarking that the plantar would be called to account by the reformers in England for letting the negroes dance on Christmas day. . . . Mr. Graham told me there would be a rebellion in the island if any attempt was made to curtail the enjoyments of the blacks, even on religious principles.[28]

Williams brought up in his discussion an instance of the effects of acculturation on the slave. The assimilated or possibly mixed-blood slaves did not wish to participate in the African dances. The importance of these celebrations is alluded to in the stated fear of rebellion if the events were prohibited. Here the drum is attributed with a kind of significance and in this context respected as an element of black culture.

Michael Scott witnessed a funeral while in Jamaica sometime after 1806. The following is taken from his published work, *Tom Cringle's Log* of 1833.

> a negro funeral came past, preceded by a squad of . . . black ragabands, singing and playing on gumbies, or African drums, made out of pieces of hollow trees, about six feet long, with slains braced over them, each carried by one man, while another beats it with his open hands.

A wake is later described.

> No white person ever broke in on these orgies . . . the negroes are very averse to their doing so . . . a loud drumming which, as I came nearer, every now and then sunk into a low murmuring roll, when a strong bass voice would burst forth into a wild recitative; which succeeded a loud piercing chorus of female voices, during which the drums were beaten with great vehemence; this was succeeded by another solo, and so on. . . . Before the door a circle was formed by about twenty women . . . sitting on the floor, and swaying their bodies to and fro, while they sung in chorus the wild dirge already mentioned, the words of which I could not make out; in the center of the circle sat four men playing on the gumbies, or the long drum formerly described, while a fifth stood behind them, with a conch-shell, which kept sounding at intervals.[29]

Large drums are described here as well as singing, a circle of participants, and a setting that is, to say the least, quite foreign to Michael Scott. The use of the drum was obviously still integrated into black life in the Caribbean in the early nineteenth century, and the drum's use, based on this observer, was more African than not.

## American Writers

Thomas Wentworth Higginson was an ordained minister and graduate of the Harvard Divinity School whose interest in social causes included anti-slavery and women's rights. He commanded the first black regiment of the Civil War, the First South Carolina Volunteers, and recorded his impressions in "Leaves from an Officer's Journal" of 1864 and "Army Life in a Black Regiment" of 1870, that were published in the *Atlantic Monthly*. Higginson is also known for his association with poet Emily Dickinson, as a mentor to her who encouraged her to share her work with the world. Higginson has described both religious and secular music among the black soldiers he led. Examples from his "Army Life" will be discussed in Chapter Five.

George Washington Cable's chronicles of African music and dance in Congo Square in New Orleans are among the best known and most often quoted. He wrote "The Dance in Place Congo" and "Creole Slave Songs" that each appeared in *The Century Magazine* in 1886. Both articles are detailed accounts of the life styles of the diverse African population of New Orleans, that was notable for the many gradations along the color line, from quadroons to octaroons, and beliefs that included vodou. Cable quotes local expressions and song lyrics in French Creole with notated music. Densely illustrated, these articles show the work of artist E. W. Kemble, who was known for his depictions of African Americans. The depictions, both artistic and literary, are caricatured, and there is some of the fantastic in the author's use of such superlatives as "frenzy" and "madness" in his presentations of dance, and in the artist's portrayal of blacks playing drums by using a large bone as a drum stick. These eccentricities weaken the perceived objectivity of the works and lessen their usefulness.[30]

In 1885 Charles Dudley Warner, Mark Twain's associate who was mentioned earlier, witnessed and recorded a vodou ceremony in New Orleans in a private home, where a friend helped him gain entrance. Although he does not mention the drum, there is much that is rhythmic in his description.

> The colored woman at the side of the altar began a chant in a low, melodious voice. It was the weird and strange "Danse Calinda." . . . The chant grew, the single line was enunciated in stronger pulsations, and other voices joined in the wild refrain,
>
> Danse Calinda, boudoum, boudoum!
> Danse Calinda, boudoum, boudoum!
>
> bodies swayed, the hands kept time in soft patting, and the feet in muffled accentuation. The Voudou arose, removed his slippers . . . and then

> began in the open space a slow measured dance, a rhythmical shuffle, with more movement of the hips than of the feet, backward and forward, round and round, but accelerating his movement as the time of the song quickened and the excitement rose in the room.

Warner continues:

> While the wild chanting, the rhythmic movement of hands and feet, the barbarous dance, and the fiery incantations were at their height, it was difficult to believe that we were in a civilized city of an enlightened republic. Nothing indecent occurred in word or gesture, but it was so wild and bizarre that one might easily imagine he was in Africa or in hell.[31]

This late-nineteenth-century account is interesting for the feeling or impression an African ceremony imparted on Warner the witness. Much like Isaac Holmes' 1821 account, which seems out of place for the time, Warner's obviously chance experience is surprising. Rhythm, and by implication, the drum, is everywhere in this account and is a statement on the ubiquity of rhythm in African diasporic practices.

In 1877 journalist Lafcadio Hearn went to New Orleans on assignment from the *Cincinnati Commercial* newspaper to write a series on Louisiana politics. He had already written pieces on the life of urban blacks and is known today for his vignettes on African American culture. In New Orleans he witnessed, in 1885, black dances that he described in a letter to a friend.

> Yes, I have seen them dance, but they danced the Congo, and sang a purely African song. . . . As for the dance—in which the women do not take their feet off the ground—it is as lascivious as is possible. The men dance very differently, like savages leaping in the air.[32]

Again, here is an account of performance that was "purely African" but without mention of the drum. Hearn was known as an orientalist, a teller of tales based on personal experience in so-called exotic places. He lived and married, for example, in Japan. This look at the types of individuals who recorded African American music and commented on its aspects, in positive and negative ways, suggests the preponderance of drums in American culture up to the late nineteenth century, as described in the accounts, and the apparent African, or at least unacculturated, nature of the music and dance. In the next chapter I will look in closer detail at the performances to reveal what the performers were actually doing.

## Notes

1 Benjamin Franklin, *The Writings of Benjamin Franklin*, Vol. 6, ed. Albert Henry Smith (New York: Macmillan, 1906). See Eileen Southern, *African American Traditions in Song, Sermon, Tale, and Dance, 1600s–1920* (Westport, CT: 1990), 2.
2 Thomas Jefferson, *Notes on the State of Virginia* (Paris: Publisher, 1872). See Dena Epstein, *Sinful Tunes and Spirituals: Black Folk Music to the Civil War* (Chicago: University of Chicago Press, 1977), 34.
3 J. Hector St. John de Crevecoeur, "More Letters from an American Farmer," in *Sketches of Eighteenth Century America*, ed. Henri L. Bourdin (New Haven: Yale University Press, 1925), 96, 148. See Traditions 2.
4 Benjamin Rush, "Diseases Peculiar to the Negroes," *American Museum* 4 (1788), 81–2. See *Sinful Tunes* 42.
5 John Pierpont, *Journal* (New York: Pierpont Morgan Library, 1805). See *Sinful Tunes* 84.
6 Charles Dickens, *American Notes* (1842).
7 Frederick Law Olmsted, *A Journey in the Seaboard Slave States, with Remarks on Their Economy* (New York: C. P. Mason Brothers, 1859). See Traditions citation no. 321.
8 Mark Twain and Charles Dudley Warner, *The Gilded Age: A Tale of Today* (Hartford: American Publishing Company, 1892). See *Traditions* 14.
9 Rudyard Kipling, *American Notes* (Philadelphia: Henry Altemus, 1899). See Traditions 78.
10 Charles Peabody, "Notes on Negro Music," *Journal of American Folk Lore* 16 (July 1903), 148–52. See Traditions citation no. 2109.
11 Le Page du Pratz, *Histoire de la Louisianne* (Paris: De Bure l'aine, 1758). See *Sinful Tunes* 32.
12 Matthew Gregory Lewis, *Journal of a West India Proprietor, Kept during a Residence in the Island of Jamaica* . . . (London: J. Murray, 1834). See Lynn Emery, *Black Dance in the United States from 1615 to 1970* (Princeton: Princeton University Press, 1972).
13 Marly, Marly, *Or, a Planter's Life in Jamaica* (Glasgow: R. Griffin, 1828). See *Sinful Tunes* 53.
14 John Riland, *Memoirs of a West-India Planter* (London: Hamilton, Adams, 1828). See *Sinful Tunes* 10.
15 Patience Pennington [Elizabeth W. Allston Pringle], *A Woman Rice Planter* (New York: Macmillan, 1913). See Traditions citation 1892.
16 I use the term doctor in a general sense, realizing that for many this moniker was self-defined.
17 Alexander Falconbridge, *An Account of the Slave Trade on the Coast of Africa* (London: J. Phillips, 1788). See *Sinful Tunes* 9.
18 John Allen Wyeth, *With Sabre and Scalpel* (New York: Publisher, 1914). See *Sinful Tunes* 96.
19 James Eights, quoted in Joel Munsell in Collections. The Albany Common Council prohibited Pinkster Day possibly after 1811 according to Joel Munsell in Collections on the History of Albany. (Albany: 1867). See *Black Dance* 142.
20 William Smith, *A New Voyage to Guinea: Describing the Customs, Manners, Soil, Climate, Habits, Buildings, Education. . . .* (London: J. Nourse, 1744).
21 Richard Jobson, *The Golden Trade; or, a Discovery of the River Gambia, and the Golden Trade of the Aethiopians . . . Set Downe as They Were Collected in Travelling, Part of the Yeares, 1620 and 1621* (London: N. Okes, 1623).

22 Jean Baptiste Labat, *Nouveau Voyage aux Isles de l'Amerique. . . .* (The Hague, 1726).
23 John Ferdinand Da Iziel Smyth, *A Tour in the United States of America. . . .* (London: C. Robinson, 1784). See *Sinful Tunes* 40.
24 Nicholas Owen, *Journal of a Slave-Dealer: "A View of Some Remarkable Incedents in the Life of Nics: Owen on the Coast of Africa and America from the Year 1746 to the Year 1757"* (Boston: Houghton Mifflin, 1930). See *Black Dance* 3.
25 William Beckford, *A Descriptive Account of the Island of Jamaica. . . .* (London: T. & J. Egerton, 1790). See *Black Dance* 18.
26 Edwards Bryan, *The History, Civil and Commercial, of the British Colonies in the West Indies. . . .* (London: J. Stockdale, 1793–1801).
27 Albert Baron von Sack, *A Narrative of a Voyage to Surinam; of a Residence There during 1805, 1806, and 1807; and of the Author's Return to Europe by the Way of North America* (London: W. Bulmer, 1810). See *Sinful Tunes* 51.
28 Cynric R. Williams, *A Tour through the Island of Jamaica, from the Western to the Eastern End, in the Year 1823* (London: Hunt and Clarke, 1826).
29 Michael Scott, *Tom Cringle's Log* (Edinburgh: W. Blackwood and Sons, 1833). See *Sinful Tunes* 75. Dena Epstein makes the comment that in this account the "persistence of African cultural patterns until well into the nineteenth century is striking."
30 See Francis Martin Jr., "Edward Windsor Kemble, a Master of Pen and Ink," *American Art Review* (February, 1976). See also *Black Dance* 162. and *Sinful Tunes* xvii.
31 Charles Dudley Warner, *Studies in the South and West, with Comments on Canada* (Hartford: American Publishing Company, 1904). See *Black Dance* 170.
32 Lafcadio Hearn, *Two Years in the French West Indies* (New York: Harper, 1890). See *Black Dance* 165.

# 2 Performance Practices

It is essential to understand the ways in which the drum was perceived in the Americas and used by African Americans. In the previous chapter I provided a glimpse of the individuals who left behind the records. In this chapter I will survey the actual physical settings for drum performance, revealing again the point of view of the observers but also the ways in which African Americans performed and for what reasons. After a focus on the viewers and the users, the relationships between these two groups—fear, threat, racism, ignorance, intrigue—might be further revealed. What is most interesting is not so much who the African was or what the drum was, as what the person and the drum represented during the slave era. The sheer variety of descriptions as well as the seeming contradictions of drums and other instruments, absent in some settings but continuing in others, makes clear an inconsistency in the idea that the drum was totally banned in North America. The expressed interest of those whites who reported performances and ceremonies well into the late nineteenth century shows that, within all of the aspects of assimilation that African Americans underwent, some conspicuously African-like practices continued.

## The Seventeenth and Eighteenth Centuries

Early records of the use of the drum by blacks outside of Africa come from accounts from slave ships, such as that of ship's surgeon Alexander Falconbridge in the previous chapter. Another early account dates from 1580 in the records of the Dutch West India Company, which instructed ship authorities to provide wooden drums in order to keep the slaves in "bouyant spirits."[1] As mentioned earlier, Europeans found the singing, dancing, and drumming compelling but missed hearing a tune that might be familiar to their ears. A description from 1647 from Barbados mentions the apparent lack of a tune again but also takes note of what was emphasized in the place of it.

> In the afternoon on Sundays, they have their musicke, which is of kettle drums, and those of several sises; upon the smallest the best musician playes, and the others come in as Chorasses: the drum all men know, has but one tone and therefore varietie of tunes have little to due in this musicke; and yet so strangely they varie their time, as 'tis a pleasure to the most curious eayes, and it was to me one of the strangest noyses that ever I heard made of one tune' and if they had the varietie of tune, which gives the greater scope in musicke, as they have of time, they would do wonders in that Art.[2]

Here Richard Ligon was impressed with the rhythms and in how the performers "varie their time," almost to the exclusion of the need for any melody. Ligon hinted at what is the essence of much African and African American music, what has been described as a "dominance of percussion."[3] Ligon's language falls all over itself in explanation. He observed that the drum has no tune and "yet so strangely" the time changes, that is "they varie their time" so that if the African were a tunesmith they would "do wonders." Possibly Ligon was hearing a tune played by each drum or a composite melody produced by many drums, as is common in African music, but had never experienced this before and was at a loss for words.

That African practices had arrived in the new hemisphere early on is clear from the testimony. What solidifies these accounts is the existence of physical evidence. Sir Hans Sloane, whose account will appear in the next chapter, left behind an African drum that was found in Virginia in the mid-eighteenth century and that exists today in the collection of the British Museum. This instrument has been compared to other existing drums from the west coast of Africa, also from earlier times (see Illustration 2.1).

In an account from New York, Dutch burghers and farmers who traveled to the city witnessed drumming by an African said to be 125 years old who "did most of the beating" to African songs.[4] Another North American account comes from the judicial records of Somerset County, Maryland, 1701 to 1711, in which there is a complaint that slaves were "Drunke on the Lords Day beating their Negro drums by which they call considerable Number of Negroes together in some Certaine places."[5] Many accounts point out the dancing and drumming that took place on Sundays as this appears to have been the only universal day of rest for the slave. The conflict then between what slaveholders approved of as respectful on a Christian Sunday was up against the reality of African practices.

*Illustration 2.1* "Virginia Drum." 1735.

Source: African drum from eighteenth-century Virginia. Exhibit number 1368 of the bequest of Sir Hans Sloane of 1753, the British Museum.

In 1708 John Oldmixon used similar terminology to describe the slave music of Barbados that Richard Ligon used in 1647 as described earlier. "They have two Musical Instruments, like Kettle Drums, for each Company of Dancers, with which they make a very barbarous Melody."[6] It is interesting that both men describe a "kettle drum" shape or at least relate the African drums to this and that they both addressed the "tune" or "melody" or lack thereof, in the music they heard.

A description from an anonymous English soldier in Guadeloupe in 1763 identified a drum-like instrument, the differences between the acculturated and "raw" slaves, and the variations in musical outcomes of these two groups.

> Some of the Mulattoes can play indifferently well on the violin; they have likewise a kind of tabou, it hath but one head, and all round the hoop are fixed small pieces of tin; the manner of playing is to hold the

> instrument with one hand, and beat on the parchment head with the fingers of the other, according to the tune of the violin; others are singing to the tune; and some beat on the boards at the side of the hut in which the hall is kept, and others will clap their hands, all which instrumental and vocal music together makes a most hideous concert. Their chief dances are minuets and jigs, and some of the Creole slaves will dance an minuet tolerably well, after the French mode. . . . The women will dance down two or three men in a jig.[7]

A wedding is also described.

> But these weddings, as well as balls, are only kept up by the Creole slaves; the raw negroes, have not wherewith to do so, but assemble in another part of the plantation, and direct themselves after their own country manner. Their chief instrument of music is a small cask, on one end is fastened a sheep or goat skin, with the hair off, and the musician sits across like Bacchus, beating on the head with his hands; all the assembly gather around him, and sing to the tune which he beats, which indeed is all at random, and the instrumental and vocal musick make a most terrible discord.[8]

The drum-like instrument, the tabou, is, of course, a reference to the tambourine, a "hoop" around which "are fixed small pieces of tin." The mulatoes or creoles utilize the violin and dance the minuet "after the French mode." In contrast are the music and dancing of the slaves who performed "after their own country manner" with the drum. The rhythms and song of the Africans were "all at random," which was certainly a reflection of the listener's consternation and possibly a reference to the improvisatory nature of what he heard.

A traveler to Jamaica around the same time, in 1788, also reported dancing that exhibited affectations of the European but with suggestions to movement and rhythm that could be African in origin.

> At Christmas the slaves are allowed three days holiday. . . . The . . . negroes and mulattoes pay a visit to the white people . . . one of them attends with a fiddle, and the men dress in the English mode, with cocked hats, cloth coats, Holland shirts, and pumps. They dance minuets with the mulattoes and other brown women, imitating the motion and steps of the English, but with a degree of affection. . . . But their own way of dancing is droll indeed; they put themselves into strange postures, and shake their hips and great breasts to such a degree, that it is impossible to refrain from laughing, though they go through the whole performance with preferred gravity, their feet beating time remarkably

> quick; two of them generally dance together, and sometimes do not move six inches from the same place.[9]

Just like the anonymous soldier's account above, Peter Marsden here recounted both European music and dance by the slaves and African dance by the slaves. There is, by the way, no shortage of derogatory comments in this last set of descriptions. For Marsden "it is impossible to refrain from laughing," and the soldier complained that "the instrumental and vocal musick make a most terrible discord." Although no other instruments—except the violin—are mentioned in Marsden's account, he did make reference to the dancers' feet "beating time remarkably quick," an obvious reference to the rhythmic nature of the African dance of the slaves.

P. J. Laborie similarly witnessed the weekend dancing of slaves and African music and drums in Santo Domingo, the capital of the French colony that later become the Dominican Republic, but in this instance during New Year festivities.

> On Saturday or Sunday evening, the negroes are allowed to dance upon the platforms [used for drying coffee] . . . till nine o'clock . . . [on] New Year's Day. . . . The morning just begins to dawn, when a hurricane of drums, of descendent shouts, and African songs, awake the master from his slumbers. . . . [The slaves] go to dress themselves in their best cloaths; they return and begin to dance . . . the ball breaks up to give time for breakfast. . . . The dance is resumed with redoubled alacrity. . . . [In the evening] the dance rages more and more lively and swift. Every nerve is in motion, every exertion raised to the utmost. All . . . keep pace with the drums, now beating with ten-fold quickness.[10]

The author here described an all-day celebration initiated by "a hurricane of drums." Great enthusiasm is suggested as well as a type of momentum to the progress of the day that increased with the accompaniment of the drums. This presentation seems modern-day, carnival-like, as there is a suspension of normal activity and a focus on the revelry of the moment.

## The Nineteenth Century

This chapter has thus far described the drum on slave ships, at Saturday and Sunday celebrations, at Christmas and New Year's, and at a wedding. An account from Jamaica in 1809 describes a funeral in which the drum was central to the ceremony.

> At their funerals . . . is the practice of pouring libations, and sacrificing a fowl on the grave of the deceased; a tribute of respect. . . . During

> the whole of this ceremony many fantastic motions and wild gesticulations are practiced, accompanied with a suitable beat of their drums, and other rude instruments while a melancholy dirge is sung by a female, the chorus of which is performed by the whole of the other females with admirable precision, and full-toned, and not unmelodious voices. . . . When the deceased is interred, the plaintive notes of sympathy and regret are no longer heard; the drums resound with a livelier beat, the song grows animated and cheerful; dancing and apparent merriment commences, and the remainder of the night is spent in feasting.[11]

The pouring of libations and drumming implies an African foundation to the ceremony, as does the call-and-response format of the singing. The progression from the feeling of solemnity to celebration calls to mind African American funerals of the next century.

An account from 1816 supplied considerable detail concerning an ensemble of instruments that accompanied dance in the West Indies.

> The instrumental parts of the band consist of a species of drum, a kind of rattle, and the ever-delighting banjar. The first is a long hallow piece of wood, with a dried sheep skin tied over the end; the second is a calabash containing a number of small stones, fixed to a short stick which serves as the handle, and the third is a coarse and rough . . . guitar, while one negro strikes the banjar, another shakes the rattle with great force of arm; a third sitting across the body of the drum, as it lies lengthwise upon the ground, beats and kicks the sheep skin at the end, in violent exertion with his hands and heels; and a fourth sitting upon the ground at the other end, behind the man upon the drum, beats upon the wooden sides of it with two sticks. Together with these noisy sounds, numbers of the party of both sexes band forth their . . . delighting song with all possible force of lungs . . . a spectator would require only a slight aid from fancy to transport him to the savage wilds of Africa. On great occasions the band is increased by an additional number of drums, rattles, and voices.[12]

George Pinckard, in this excerpt from his *Notes on the West Indies*, identified a musical ensemble with the African drum, additional percussion, and possibly an early version of the banjo. The "noisy sounds" provided music for dancers that practically "transported" the author to the "wilds of Africa." This description confirms the functional aspect of music-for-dance, for which the drum is most commonly known.

Architect Benjamin Latrobe, whose writings were cited in the previous chapter, also provided descriptions of African instruments and their players, as well as portrayals of the dancers to the music. His account of music making in Congo Square in New Orleans dates from 21 February 1819.

> A bill was moved, I think, in the last session of the Legislature to put down the practice of dancing and shop keeping prevailing here on Sunday. . . . My accidentally stumbling upon the assembly of Negroes which I am told every Sunday afternoon meets on the Common in the rear of the city. . . . Approaching the common I heard a most extraordinary noise, which I supposed to proceed from some horse mill, the horses trampling on a wooden floor. I found, however, on emerging from the horses onto the Common, that it proceeded from a crowd of 5 or 600 persons assembled in an open space or public square. I . . . crowded near enough to see the performance. All those who were engaged in the business seemed to be blacks. I did not observe a dozen yellow faces. They were formed into circular groups in the midst of four of which, which I examined (but there were more of them), was a ring, the largest not 10 feet in diameter. In the first were two women dancing. They held each a coarse handkerchief extended by the corners in their hands, and set to each other in a miserably dull and slow figure, hardly moving their feator bodies.[13]

Latrobe's consideration of the instruments took the following form:

> The music consisted of two drums and a stringed instrument. An old man sat astride of a cylindrical drum about a foot in diameter, and beat it with incredible quickness with the edge of his hand and fingers. The other drum was an open staved thing held between the knees and beaten in the same manner. They made an incredible noise. The most curious instrument, however, was a stringed instrument which no doubt was imported from Africa. On the top of the finger board was the rude figure of a man in a sitting posture, and two pegs behind him to which the strings were fastened. The body was a calabash. It was played upon by a very little old man, apparently 80 or 90 years old.

He continued, with more observations of dancing and drumming:

> The women squalled out a burden to the playing at intervals, consisting of two notes, as the negroes, working in our cities, respond to the song of their leader. Most of the circles contained the same sort of dancers. One was larger, in which a ring of a dozen women walked, by way of dancing, round the [?] in the center. But the instruments were of a different construction. One, which from the color of the weed seemed

> new, consisted of a block cut into something of the form of a cricket bat with a long and deep mortise down the center. This thing made a considerable noise, being beaten lustily on the side by a short stick. In the same orchestra was a square drum, looking like a stool, which made an abominably loud noise; also a calabash with a round hole in it, the hole studded with brass nails, which was beaten by a woman with two short sticks.
>
> A man sung an unearthly song to the dancing which I suppose was in some African language, for it was not French, and the women screamed a detestable burden on one single note. The allowed amusements of Sunday have, it seems, perpetuated here those of Africa among its inhabitants. I have never seen anything more brutally savage, and at the same time dull and stupid, than this whole exhibition. Continuing my walk about a mile along the canal, and returning after Sunset near the same spot, the noise was still heard. There was not the least disorder among the crowd, nor do I learn on enquiry, that these weekly meetings of the negroes have ever produced any mischief.

In these four passages Latrobe makes a number of points. He witnessed music and dancing on a Sunday, as did Richard Ligon and P. J. Laborie. Five to six hundred people are quite large numbers, considering that these were slaves. If the stereotype regarding the leniency of slaveholders in New Orleans is true, this assessment certainly reinforces the idea. The participants danced in circular groups; the significance of this will be seen in Chapter Four in the discussion of the religious ring shout.

One important point made by Latrobe is his mention in the first section of how the two women danced: "They held each a coarse handkerchief extended by the corners in their hands." Latrobe's description of the handkerchiefs has a striking resemblance to an unattributed folk painting from about 1775, which shows two black women dancing while each are holding the corners of a large piece of white cloth. Although these two accounts, one verbal and the other pictorial, are in no way related, it is as if Latrobe has described the women in the painting *The Old Plantation.* The dress of the women in the painting, in particular their head wraps, have been attributed to Yoruba cloth from West Africa. The artist depicts one man playing a drum and another playing a banjo-like instrument with what appears to be a gourd for a body.

Another striking comment is found in the second part of the same sentence and describes the dancing of the two women—how they "set to each other in a miserably dull and slow figure, hardly moving their feat or bodies." Latrobe was explaining how the women "set" a "figure" or danced in a manner that was a slow shuffling motion. Similarly he described in the second passage how "a ring of a dozen women walked, by way of dancing," which also calls to mind rather conservative body movements. Both of these representations are coincidental with other accounts of circular dancing, a number of which will be considered in Chapter Four under the topic of shouts.

The second section of this account mentions an ensemble of three instruments, two drums and a stringed instrument which together made an "incredible noise." The "curious" banjo-like stringed instrument was drawn by the author as was a cylindrical drum, showing its position between the legs, and a percussion instrument, possibly a clave, which is also described earlier, and a type of box drum.[14]

Latrobe twice mentions women singing. "The women squalled out a burden to the playing at intervals" and "the women screamed a detestable burden." In the first the author adds how the singing was part of a call-and-response pattern with the instruments, "as the negroes, working in our cities, respond to the song of their leader."

In the last section the man mentioned sang "an unearthly song to the dancing which I suppose was in some African language." He continues: "I have never seen anything more brutally savage, and at the same time dull and stupid, than this whole exhibition," and concludes that for all of this activity there was "not the least disorder." Benjamin Latrobe's description of this so-called savage display contains ten specific references to African performance practices and is one of the most valuable, in the literature, for its concentration. The condescension here in the face of these transported practices are as amazing as the evidence it presents.

Another detailed description of dance and drumming, by Cynric Williams from 1823 in Jamaica, presents the John Canoe, a Christmas ceremony known throughout the Caribbean. Williams mentions the "gombay" drum in the context of this elaborate costumed dance.

> First come eight or ten young girls marching before a man dressed up in a mask with a grey beard and long flowing hair, who carried the model of a house on his head. This house is called the Jonkanoo, and the bearer of it is generally chosen for his superior activity in dancing. He first saluted his master and mistress, and then capered about with an astonishing agility and violence. The girls also dance without changing their position, moving their elbows and knees, and keeping tune with the calabashes filled with small stones. One of the damsels betraying, as it seemed, a little too much friskiness in her gestures, was reproved by her companions for her impedance. . . . All this time an incessant hammering was kept up on the gombay, and the cotta (a Windsor chair taken from the piazza to serve as a secondary drum) and the Jonkanoo's

> attendant went about collecting money from the dancers and from the white people.[15]

Much like the North American Pinkster Day, the Caribbean John Canoe is a creation of the New World. Both borrowed dance and drumming from Africa and were based around the Christian holidays of the Pentecost and Christmas.

James Alexander provided an account of a celebration on a sugar plantation in British Guyana in 1833. This is another, but later, account that describes both acculturated and African performance at once.

> Two or three musicians . . . with fiddle, tambourine and drum, strike up some lively jigs, at the same time thumping the floor vigorously with their heels. . . . Outside the house, in the moonlight, a musician seated himself with his drum on the grass, and commenced singing an African air, when a circle of men and women, linked hand in hand, danced round him with rattling seeds on their legs and joined in the chorus.[16]

And another description comparing the African and assimilated celebrations of slaves comes from Johan Nissen from his experiences on the island of St. Thomas about 1838.

> It is the custom here, especially among the coloured persons, to celebrate the old year's night with music, dancing, singing, and shout, making a great noise. . . . Some of them . . . put up a tent of cocoanut leaves, and dance there during the night. Many of them again dance in their own rooms, which are certainly very small, and are so full that the dancers have scarcely room to move. The dances of the negroes are of one sort: turning and moving about—they have no regular dances. Their principal instrument is called the [Gombee]. This is a small barrel, the bottom of which being taken out, a goat skin is drawn over the rim. They must have one on purpose continually knocking on this Gombee, which sounds very hard and makes a great deal of noise. But this music and sort of dancing is more a custom amongst the lower class of negroes and slaves, for amongst the well educated persons they have learnt dancing, have very good music, and often give balls like the white inhabitants.[17]

Both Alexander and Nissen present early nineteenth-century observations of an evolution in performance with references to European practices. Most importantly we see a culture in transition.

The material discussed thus far brings to the mid-nineteenth century accounts of the use of the African drum with dance in the Caribbean and North America. The reports show the settings for drumming and dance and the similarities between the mainland and the islands. Along with those descriptions presented earlier, which included late-nineteenth-century observations of drumming, the present chapter, by focusing on portrayals of the types of events and the dances and instruments used, makes clear the varied use of the drum in the Americas. With this introduction to the interested parties and the broad base of contexts for the drum's use, the next chapter will look at the stereotype of the ban on the drum during slavery and what that has meant in reality.

## Notes

1 Cornelis Christian Goslinga, *The Dutch in the Caribbean and on the Wild Coast, 1580–1680* (Gainesville: University of Florida Press, 1971). See Dena Epstein, *Sinful Tunes and Spirituals: Black Folk Music to the Civil War* (Chicago: University of Chicago Press, 1977), 10.
2 Richard Ligon, *A True & Exact History of the Island of Barbados* (London: H. Moseley, 1657). See *Sinful Tunes* 26.
3 This term is used by Richard Alan Waterman in "African Influence on the Music of the Americas," *International Congress of Americanists*, 1949.
4 Herbert Asbury, *The French Quarter* (Garden City, NY: 1938). See Lynn Emery, *Black Dance in the United States from 1615 to 1970* (Princeton: Princeton University Press, 1972), 140.
5 Russell Menard, "Slave Population," in *William and Mary Quarterly* (1975).
6 John Oldmixon, *The British Empire in America, Containing the History of the Discovery, Settlement, Progress and Present State of All the British Colonies on the Continent and Islands of America* (London: J. Brotherton, 1708). See *Sinful Tunes* 31.
7 Anonymous, *A Soldier's Journal, Containing a Popular Description of . . . with an Entertaining Account of the Islands of Guadeloupe, Dominique, etc.* (London: E. and C. Dilly, 1770). See *Sinful Tunes* 81.
8 Ibid.
9 Peter Marsden, *An Account of the Island of Jamaica; with Reflections on the Treatment, Occupation, and Provisions of the Slaves . . . By a Gentleman Lately Resident on a Plantation* (Newcastle: S. Hodgaon, 1788). See *Sinful Tunes* 83.
10 P. J. Laborie, *The Coffee Planter of Saint Domingo; with an Appendix . . .* (London: T. Cadell and W. Davies, 1798). See *Sinful Tunes.*
11 John Stewart, *An Account of Jamaica, and Its Inhabitants: By a Gentleman, Long Resident in the West Indies* (Kingston, Jamaica. 1809). See *Sinful Tunes* 65.
12 George Pinckard, *Notes on the West Indies* (London: Baldwin, Cradock and Joy, 1816). See *Sinful Tunes* 61.
13 Benjamin Henry Boneval Latrobe, *Impressions Respecting New Orleans: Diary & Sketches, 1818–1820* (New York: Columbia University Press, 1951). See *Black Dance* 158.
14 "Drawing of a Banjo by Benjamin Latrobe." 1819. Sketches from the manuscript journal of Benjamin Latrobe. Entry for Feb'y 21st, 1819, from New Orleans,

describing "the assembly of Negro . . . every Sunday . . . on the Common." The Papers of Benjamin Henry Latrobe. Maryland Historical Society. Dena J. Epstein, *Sinful Tunes and Spirituals: Black Folk Music to the Civil War* (Chicago: University of Chicago Press, 1977), 98.

15 Williams, Cynric R. *A Tour Through the Island of Jamaica, from the Western to the Eastern End in the Year 1823* (London: Hunt and Clark, 1826). See *Black Dance* 33.

16 Sir James Edward Alexander, *Transatlantic Sketches, Comprising Visits to the Most Interesting Scenes in North and South America, and the West Indies: With Notes on Negro Slavery and Canadian Emigration* (Philadelphia: Key and Biddle, 1833). See *Sinful Tunes* 87.

17 Johan Peter Nissen, *Reminiscences of a 46 Years' Residence in the Island of St. Thomas, in the West Indies* (Nazareth, PA: Senseman, 1838). See *Sinful Tunes* 88.

# 3 The Drum's Prohibition Through Time

It is commonly known that the African drum was banned in the Americas during the slave era. It was said that the drum was to be feared by slave masters for its use as an instrument of communication for slave uprisings. The idea of the black male slave inducing a drum to talk calls to mind an image of the slave's latent capacity for subterfuge and insurrection. The fear of a potential, the unfamiliar and exotic power of the slave, has fueled a great myth.

The use of the drum in the Americas as a communication tool in uprisings is vastly outweighed by the drum's use in other unrelated functions of communication in social and religious contexts. Slaveholders may not have acknowledged the cultural link between African music, dance, and religious practices but they set out to prohibit them all in many areas of the Americas. It is true that the war drum, universal to many cultures, was something to be feared, but both Europeans and Americans, based on their own accounts, show that the African drum was not merely an instrument of war. The documentary evidence presents a contradiction. The drum is at once described as an accessory to revolt and as an integral part of African American culture.

The African drum was often described in dance performances that took place among slaves on holidays and special occasions. The drum was also described in religious ceremonies and in ritual vodou. That the drum continued in use, and was talked about by observers, suggests that the ban didn't work. What does it mean that there are so few accounts of the drum being used in revolts? Did the ban in fact work so well that there was a deterrent effect, or was it that there was no African war drum to begin with?

This chapter will interpret the available historical literature on the prohibition of the African drum in the Americas. Accounts and examples will be presented by topic, chronologically within each, with an eye towards establishing any patterns or trends that can be gleaned from the literature. Because of the nature of the evidence, and this structure, the story will move about in time and place. North America will be considered within the context of the New World African American diaspora. Probably half of the descriptions and accounts of performances considered here come from the Caribbean, during the colonial era, with most of the rest originating from North America. Although the focus here is on North America there is a relationship with the Caribbean regarding slavery and black Americans in general that will become evident. The relevant historiography will be discussed after the documentary evidence has been presented. This will allow the reader to view the materials in an order that would have otherwise been organized by author or time period.

## Drums in Revolts

Sir Hans Sloane penned one early reference to the use of the drum in revolts in the Americas. He was physician to the Duke of Albemarle and visited Jamaica in 1687. After his return to England in 1689 he wrote about his travels.

> The Negroes . . . formerly on their Festivals were allowed the use of trumpets after their Fashion, and Drums made of a piece of a hollow Tree, covered on one end with any green Skin, and stretched with Thouls or Pins. But making use of these in their Wars at home in Africa, it was thought to much inciting them to Rebellion, and so they were prohibited by the Customs of the Island.[1]

This is an isolated account for this time and place in terms of the reference to rebellion, but Sloane's words make three important points. He mentions slave festivals, he describes in specific terms the handmade drums that he witnessed, and he refers to the use of the drum in a context of violence. The best-known instance of the use of the drum in a revolt in North America was the Stono rebellion of 1739. The following is an excerpt from an account of the South Carolina incident.

> On the 9th day of September last being Sunday which is the day the Planters allow them to work for themselves, Some Angola Negroes assembled, to the number of Twenty; at a place called Stonehow. . . . Several Negroes joyned them, they calling out Liberty, marched on with Colours displayed, the two Drums beating, pursuing all the white people they met with, and killing Man Woman and Child. . . . They increased every minute by new Negroes coming to them, so that they were above Sixty, some say a hundred, on which they halted in a field, and set to dancing, Singing and beating Drums, to draw more Negroes

> to them, thinking they were now victorious over the whole Province, having marched ten miles & burnt all before them without opposition.[2]

In the years following the Stono insurrection laws were passed in South Carolina and Georgia specifically prohibiting the drum. The Slave Act of 1740, in South Carolina, sought to forbid "wooden swords, and other mischievous and dangerous weapons, or using or keeping of drums, horns, or other loud instruments, which may call together, or give sign or notice to one another of their wicked designs or purposes."[3] The Georgia law used similar language.

> And as it is absolutely necessary to the safety of this province, that all due care be taken to restrain the wondering and meeting of negroes, and other slaves, at all times, and more especially on Saturday nights, Sundays, and other holidays, and their using and carrying mischievous and dangerous weapons, or using and keeping drums, horns, or other loud instruments, which may call together or give sign or notice to one another of their wicked designs or intentions . . . and whatsoever master or owner or overseer shall permit or suffer his or their slave or slaves at any time hereafter to beat drums, blow horns, or other loud instruments . . . shall forfeit thirty shillings sterling for every such offense.[4]

In these two laws drums and horns are represented as an ancillary to weapons. The Georgia law plainly states that these instruments may be used to "call together or give sign or notice to one another." It is interesting that both of these laws use the terms "mischievous and dangerous weapons" and "wicked designs."[5] The fear of the use of the drum as an instrument of communication was clearly articulated.

These laws single out the drum and remove it from the context or situation where the instrument may have been used, to portray the drum as an instrument of revolt. The original context may as well have been festive or spiritual. Herein lies the apparent reason for such generalizations on the part of observers: since the real intent was not understood, the worst was presumed.

The only other revolt on record, to this writer's knowledge, where the drum was utilized was the Louisiana revolt of 1811 in St. John the Baptist Parish. This insurrection has been called the largest in the history of North America. "Between 300 and 500 slaves, armed with pikes, hoes, and axes but few firearms, marched on New Orleans with flags flying and drums beating."[6]

This insurrection is separated from the Stono rebellion by seventy-two years. These two accounts are similar in their depiction of slaves marching with "colours displayed" and marching with drum accompaniment. The Stono account describes a separate use of the drum for dance and to call together more slaves to participate in the action. In fact, one possible difference between the Stono and Louisiana rebellions, based on their descriptions, was that in the later Louisiana revolt drums were used for marching only and not for dance and communication. This could be taken as a sign of assimilation and a retreat from earlier African practices. Repressive laws like those that were passed after the Stono rebellion also occurred in the years following the Louisiana revolt, due to this and a number of other conspiracies that occurred in the late eighteenth century and early nineteenth century. These revolts, where there is no mention of the use of the drum, will be discussed later in this chapter.

During the slave era Africans in the Americas developed new dances that included the religious shout, the secular buck and wing and buzzard lope, and original styles of music such as the spirituals, all without the sanctioned use of the drum. Most of the drum accounts in the literature speak within the context of secular dance. Many of the rest describe religious events. The documentary accounts are strangely mute on the most feared use of the drum in revolt.

## Fear of Revolt

Dance and any meeting of blacks for celebrations or religious purposes became the code words for the fear of revolt. Although the instrument was not called by name, often the context made the events clear, and often the drum was present. An account from 1654 by Adrien Dessales on the island of Martinique describes the prohibition of a dance called Kalenda (also Calenda). The Conseil Souverain de Martinique issued an ordinance on May 4, 1654, against "danses et assemblees de negres." The ordinance was later restated to include the dance by name. Although the ordinance does not refer to drums, Dessales states that the Calenda was danced to the accompaniment of a drum called banza. Roughly translated from the original French, the drums were "often a cask or barrel, sometimes the first piece of wood they could find; it is a dance most lascivious in timing." Further incidents led to the creation of Article 16 of the Code Noir of 1685 that prohibited gatherings of slaves, day or night, on or off the property of their masters. The prohibition was restated again on August 5, 1758 and on May 23, 1772.[7]

An account from 1758 in Louisiana by Le Page du Pratz, a colonial planter, links dance with the potential for revolt.

> Nothing is more to be dreaded than to see the Negroes assemble together on Sundays, since, under pretence of Calinda, or the dance, they

> sometimes get together to the number of three or four hundred, and make a kind of Sabbath, which it is always prudent to avoid; for it is in those tumultuous meetings that they . . . plot their rebellions.[8]

Here du Pratz mentions the Calenda by name, links it to "a kind of Sabbath" and concludes that insurrections are planned under these circumstances.

These two accounts show the associations made by writers regarding the types of activities carried out by slaves. The Calenda, which is well documented as a social dance, was described here in the context of both religion and rebellion.[9] These descriptions, although they do not mention the drum by name, do talk about fundamentally African-styled dance, for which the drum was probably present. In this sense the language of these colonial era writers is coded. Some of the following examples will show a similar distance from saying that there was a fear of revolt, or that banned instruments were being used or that restricted practices were taking place, in favor of indirect language or a condescending tone. These accounts will also show the different forms of what amounted to the selective prohibition of African culture in the Americas.

An early general prohibition against gatherings of slaves in North America was a Maryland act in 1695. In 1723 the Assembly again enacted laws prohibiting the large meetings of negroes on "Sabbath and other Holydays."[10] Barbados adopted prohibitions by 1699 that stated: "Whatsoever Master, &c. shall suffer his Negro or Slave at any time to beat Drums, blow Horns, or use any other loud instruments, or shall not cause his Negro Houses once a Week to be search'd, and if any such things be there found, to be burnt . . . he shall forfeit 40 s. Sterling."[11] Like the Georgia law that was instated sometime after the Stono Rebellion, this law provides for a cash fine for any offender (the fine for disobeying the Georgia law was thirty shillings sterling). A search provision was also instituted in South Carolina, where the constables of Charlestown would dispense crowds of Negroes and "enter into any house . . . to search for such slaves."[12]

On the island of St. Kitts in 1711 and 1722, slave acts prohibited "holding dangerous assemblies or from communication at a distance by beating drums or blowing horns."[13] In Jamaica in 1717, a slave act also prohibited meetings with drums and horns, but slaves could congregate for "any innocent amusement."[14] As in the Sloane account, there appears to have been little difference between what looked like "dangerous assemblies" or "innocent amusement" on the part of observers.

There is one account of the use of the drum by blacks for nonviolent purposes, and its presumed use to call an insurrection, that comes from the Mosquito Shore in present-day Honduras in 1787. Colonel Edward Marcus Despard, on a mission on behalf of the English crown to oversee the settlement of, and allotment of land parcels in, Mosquito, left an affidavit of his activities there in defense of allegations against him for misconduct. One of the incidents described involves the detainment of Joshua Jones, a "person of colour," by local magistrates because his land claim, approved by Despard, conflicted with an earlier unauthorized claim made by another settler who was white. In his description of the incident, one informant described under oath how Jones presented no "opposition" and went on to add "nor did I see any appearance of such a disposition among any of the people of colour." Jones was not only a land owner but possessed eleven slaves of his own. Despard makes the point earlier in his account that as governor he had been made aware of the fact that "people of colour" received "frequent insults" and were put under "hardships" by various other settlers of Mosquito Shore. Despard continues his assessment.

The people found themselves entirely excluded from the privileges of British subjects; and from the means of making a livelihood and even of having a house to live in; and that they were so grossly abused by persons in the character of Magistrates as even to have common walking sticks forcibly taken out of their hands and thrown into the river, when they were walking peaceably along the street.

Far from being an aggressive presence the "free blacks & mulattoes," among whom Despard divided "lots in the town" with other white settlers, were subjected to common abuse. Yet the same informant who had earlier escorted Jones under custody relates the following incident.

> I was one of the numbers that took the first guard and remained till near three o'clock of Sunday morning; during all my stay I did not see any appearance of a rescue from the people of colour, but all was peace and quietness the whole time, excepting one small mistake that we Gentlemen made. Our Mr. Edward Davis and Mr. Lawless by taking a negro's gombay for a drum which alarmed the gentlemen so much that Mr. Davis called to arms; Mr. Jackson went upon a reconnoitering party and soon released the gentlemen from their fears, informing the company that it was a few negroes diverting themselves playing the gombay.[15]

It is interesting here how the gombay, which is a drum, is spoken of in the sense that it is not a drum, that is, a war drum. This is certainly as removed an account in time and place as was Sir Hans Sloane's depiction from the Caribbean, mentioned at the beginning of this chapter. Though it seems that the African drum had a presumed purpose throughout the slaveholding world.

## Language and Intent

A general observation regarding these historical accounts are the superlatives that were often used to characterize witnessed events and performance scenes. Blacks held "tumultuous meetings" (du Pratz) and performed dances "lascivious in timing" (Dessales). Dessales' quote adds a sexual connotation to the dance, and as one of the following accounts shows, some observers found African dance movements offensive. This point begs the question, was there a relation between the use of African music and what was viewed as improper practices carried out between the sexes, and how were women viewed by the observers, since the Calenda that Dessales describes was danced in couples? The following account from Sir William Young's journal entry on St. Vincent in 1791 is a further example.

> In the evening I opened the ball in the great court, with a minuet with black Phillis . . . our music consisted of two excellent fiddles . . . and . . . tamborin . . . there stood up about eighteen couple. . . . This moment a new party of musicians are arrived with an African Balafo, an instrument composed of pieces of hard wood of different diameters, laid on a row over a sort of box; they beat on one or the other so as to strike out a good musical tune. They played two or three African tunes; and about a dozen girls, hearing their sound, came from huts to the great court, and began a curious and most lascivious dance, with much grace as well as action; of the last, plenty in truth.[16]

This observer certainly did not miss much. The drum here has been substituted by the balafon, an African xylophone.

There must have been a reason for this fantastic language. These writers may have been witnessing something that they had never seen before. The choice of words may as well have portrayed their shock at such exhibitions. They may have also simply been unable to put into words adequately the music and dance they were a party to. Possibly this is evidence of the cultural difference between Europeans and Africans and the standards of behavior, dress, and modesty of the two cultures. Also, because these were descriptions of slaves, a modicum of abusive language should probably be expected. Surely Young's flippant reference to "black Phillis" and the "action" of the African dance can call into question his level of respect for female slaves and bewilderment at things African.

## A Culture in Retreat

The 1740s appear to have been a watershed for the perseverance of the African ways of the slave population in North America. The negative impact of the Stono insurrection of 1739 must have been great, as witnessed by the laws that were passed in its aftermath. In 1741 the New York City slave conspiracy, which ended in the execution of thirty-one blacks, was largely the result of white hysteria pointed towards what turned out to be a biracial gang of thieves and arsonists.[17] The 1740s were also the first decade where, in the Chesapeake, the black population began to grow mainly by natural increase, suggesting that an acculturated African American population had evolved.

The tone and content of the accounts of African American culture change for North America after this time. For example, in 1749 North Carolina slaves and free blacks were prohibited from meeting "for the purpose of drinking and dancing" by the General Assembly.[18] The simplified language, as compared to that of earlier statements, is worthy of note. By this time the drum was taboo in North America, so its absence from accounts can be reconciled in terms of the idea of the coded language mentioned earlier. As some of the following descriptions show, it is also possible that the acculturation process was having the effect that European culture, songs, and dances had mixed with African forms to a greater extent.[19] The drum may have fallen into disuse because slaves were dancing more European- than African-based dances. Was the drum there all the time, and not being talked about, or had African Americans been forced, or chosen, not to use it?

## An Opposing Paradigm

Revisionist history says that in North America the drum was banned and that in the Caribbean, because slaveholders were much more free with their chattel, cultural and religious activities in general were permitted.[20] It is my contention that although the drum was not "omnipresent" in North America, it continued to be used for dance, religious events and communication. For the Caribbean, the examples presented thus far suggest that there was considerable restriction on slaves' non-work activities. In North America, African cultural practices were also under attack, but may have in fact succeeded over time to a greater extent than they have been given credit for in accounts.

Thomas Jefferys, an English geographer and mapmaker, reported a dance scene he witnessed in 1760 in the Caribbean. "The Calendoe, a sport brought from the coast of Guinea, and attended with gestures which are not entirely consistent with modesty, whence it is forbidden by the public laws of the islands."[21] Here a form of the Calenda is mentioned and in this case was supposed to have been opposed because of its immodesty, not because of its danger in revolt. Into the late eighteenth century there continued to be prohibitions against the drum in the Caribbean. In Jamaica in 1788 the New Consolidated Acts XIX, XX, and XXI declared it illegal for "slaves to assemble together, and beat their military drums, or blow their horns or shells."[22]

During this same time period in one place in North America, New Orleans, there were actually concessions being made to the rights of slaves to congregate in public. By 1786 slaves were allowed to meet on Sundays and holy days in public squares after the close of evening service.[23] In 1792, the Spanish governor of Louisiana declared by law that Sundays were for slaves' recreation. Another 1795 ordinance restricted slave dancing to Sundays.[24] In 1808, five years after the Louisiana Purchase, "Ordinances of Police" addressed slave dancing as well as censored activities at slave funerals.

> Art. 9.—As to the custom observed by several Africans and people of colour of assembling during the night, on occasion of the death of some of their acquaintance, those meetings shall be tolerated only when confined to the relations of the deceased, and when everything is conducted at them with decency. But if the tranquility of the neighborhood be disturbed with cries, singing or dancing, &c. on such occasions, the Commissary of Police and the patrols, are required to take up all persons found at such meetings after the hour of retreat.
>
> Art. 10.—It shall not be lawful for any slaves in town and suburbs to meet together for the purpose of dancing and amusing themselves, (except on Sundays, at such places only as may be therefore appointment by the Mayor, and no where else), under the penalty of ten lashes against every slave delinquent.[25]

Slave assemblies are clearly banned in Article 10, except on Sundays, with a penalty of whipping. Article 9 allows funeral ceremonies at night, as it was the "custom," and hindered the extent to which slaves could participate, in the name of "the tranquility of the neighborhood." After New Orleans became part of America, custom was allowed, but was subject to restriction. It was Congo Square in New Orleans that provided the late nineteenth century with some of its most detailed descriptions of African-based music and dance. Although New Orleans did restrict African cultural practices, the city never effectively banned such practices, because they were allowed on Sundays, and have been written about into the late nineteenth century.[26]

## Acculturation

The acculturation process continued and by the early nineteenth century accounts plainly discuss this transition.[27] In 1825 H.T. de la Beche made the following comments regarding slaves in Jamaica.

> When a negro wishes to give a dance . . . those of the old school preferring the goombay and African dances, and those of the new, fiddles,

> reels, &c. . . . The various African amusements, in which the negroes formerly took so much delight, are not now kept up with spirit, and Joncanoe himself is getting out of fashion.[28]

In 1828 Alexander Barclay gives an account, also from Jamaica, very similar to that of de la Beche. Here Barclay is discussing festivals held at the end of cane cutting.

> About twenty years ago, it was common on occasions of this kind to see the different African tribes each a distinct party, singing and dancing to the gumbay, after the rude manners of their native Africa; but this custom is now extinct. The fiddle is now the leading instrument with them, as with the white people, whom they imitate; they dance Scotch reels, and some of the better sort (who have been house servants) country dances. . . . The young people, however still indulge in some amusements on this occasion. . . . They have always with them . . . a fiddle, a drum, and a tambourine, frequently boys playing fifes.[29]

Mrs. A.C. Carmichael writes about both acculturated and African music and dance in Jamaica in about 1833.

> Sunday dances in Kingstown are not now common, but in the country they frequently occur. . . . The native African . . . dance their own African dances to the drum, while the creole negroes consider the fiddle genteeler, though of an evening among themselves they will sing, dance, and beat the drum, yet they would not produce this instrument at a grand party. Fiddles and tambourines, with triangles, are essential there.[30]

The preceding examples, all from Jamaica, make a number of points regarding the transition in slave practices. De la Beche declares that there was both the "goombay" drum and African dance, and the fiddle and "reels," but that the African ways had fallen from fashion. Barclay finds that the "gumbay" drum and "rude" dancing was extinct and that the fiddle was favored as the "leading instrument" to which "Scotch reels" and "country dances" were performed, in imitation of the whites. Carmichael reports that African dances are only found in the country in Jamaica, and not in the city of "Kingstown," and that "creole" slaves "consider the fiddle genteeler." Barclay and Carmichael both admit that the drum is still used either among the young who "indulge" or on the occasion "of an evening among themselves." These accounts show a marked contrast from earlier observations. From the more general censor on "assemblees de negres" in 1654, to the explicit language declaring the "wicked designs" inherent in the use of the drum in 1740, this later group of accounts in the 1820s and 30s makes clear the shift in black culture. The later observations also reveal a perseverance of African practices. Also, in her travels, Mrs. Carmichael came to question a missionary about prohibitions against the drum and was met with a mute response.

> I stated this to Mr. Goy, telling him that some of the negroes said the Methodists forbade their communicants dancing at all; that others said they only forbade the drum, and not the fiddle dance; while others said it was only the African dances that were disapproved of. I asked whether any of these accounts were correct,—but Mr. Goy, and afterwards Mr. Stephenson, heard me in silence, and made no answer of any kind.[31]

Well into the nineteenth century there is evidence of the continued awareness of the effect of the drum in certain situations. In 1840, as the Democratic convention was being held in Charleston, South Carolina a band sent by the New York delegation played for dignitaries at ten o'clock one evening.

> It was stopped in the midst of its performance, and forbidden to use its drums. . . . The chief of police, in full uniform, appeared on the scene . . . politely explained the rule, and the reason of it saying, "Play any music you like, if you can dispense with your drums. Their sound at this hour would arouse the whole city."[32]

It could be inferred from this occurrence that the northern band must not have thought it unusual to play at this hour, or would have done so in New York, but drums evidently had a different meaning in this Southern city at night. A periodical called *The Commercial Review of the South and West* (later *De Bow's Review*) carried an article in 1846 titled "Code Noir; or, Black Code of Louisiana," in which the Sunday dance code was discussed.[33] Another example from Louisiana in 1849 shows that slaves in St. John's Parish were restricted "from beating the drum or dancing after sundown."[34] These examples plainly show the continuance of the drum into the mid-nineteenth century.

One account from about 1884 attests to drum performance and opposition, late into the century. In a book called *The Existing Conflict* by Green Raum, the author describes controversial topics of the day such as the rise of the Ku Klux Klan and includes commentary on black fife and drum clubs in Mississippi and white censor of such activities.[35] This form of drum performance was an acculturated practice but in this instance there was still resistance to it.

## Context

There is a larger context of circumstances that must be mentioned to better understand the social climate that existed under slavery in the Americas, particularly from the mid-eighteenth to mid-nineteenth century. Beginning in the 1670s imports of African slaves to the Southern colonies of North America first increased dramatically. This fact is important to contrast with the 1654 prohibition against dances and assemblies in Martinique: that before the slave trade had even matured in North America, prohibitions had already come about in the Caribbean. By 1710 blacks had become a majority in South Carolina, and it was in 1711 that slave Acts on the island of St. Kitts restricted assemblies and the use of the drum. This juxtaposition of facts suggests the ways in which the difficulties of dealing with a transported African culture under a system of bondage were felt by Caribbean slaveholders many years earlier than in North America.

African American culture and religion had also been noticed outside of America by the late eighteenth century. In 1782 in Glasgow, Scotland, a songbook was published that included a piece which was probably influenced by black American dance. James Aird's *Selection of Scotch, English, Irish and Foreign Airs* included a "Negro Jig." This text also presented the first known printing of "Yankee Doodle."[36] Because of the fact that this Scottish book was made up in part of "foreign" music, it is at least less of a surprise to find both an African American dance tune and a Yankee tune together between its covers.

In 1794 in Philadelphia, the first independent black church in the United States was organized. Richard Allen led the Bethel African Methodist Episcopal Church in what was a reaction to the white Methodist church establishment and their limited acceptance of blacks. Reverend Allen also participated in the development of a new hymnal of music suited to the tastes of his congregation. This dramatic and carefully organized effort on the part of blacks in Philadelphia demonstrates the degree of acculturation of African Americans in some locales in North America by the late eighteenth century.[37]

Yet during this same span of years Colonel Despard's account of 1787 described the fear of revolt at the sound of a drum played by an African, and in 1788 Jamaica's New Act of Assemblybanned assemblies and drumming. It could be concluded that the acculturative process quickened in North America and that new ways developed alongside the old for African Americans. Compared to the Caribbean, was this heightened cultural development the outcome of the closer proximity of the two cultures, arguably not found in the islands, or a stricter form of slavery in the North?

The forty-year period from 1791 to 1831 encompassed a group of five of the most well-known slave revolts in history that included the Louisiana rebellion of 1811. In 1791 the Haitian revolution began, culminating in the expulsion of the French and independence in 1804. During this period of resistance there are no reports, that this author is aware of, that include the use of the drum, although African-based cultural practices were a part of this armed conflict. For example, Mackandal, a maroon chief, used poison as a weapon. This has been known to be a practice used by Africans in war as well. Mackandal's plan to poison the water of every house in the capital city was eventually betrayed. There is also the case of Hyacinth, the twenty-one year-old leader who's troops took the capital of Port-au-Prince. Hyacinth used a bull's tail as a talisman to "chase death away" from his troops. The Haitian revolutionaries by their actions showed a strong existing connection to African ways.[38]

In 1800, Gabriel Prosser was the leader of a conspiracy in Richmond, Virginia. His plot to overrun and destroy the capital city may have failed in part because he did not tap the potential revolutionary force of religion, as had been used in other revolts, but instead focused on politics. The other factor that may have brought failure was the fact that the plan was led by assimilated slaves and may have been an expression of their class at the exclusion of other slaves; it was not an inclusive action. African practices had little association to such an effort.[39]

In Denmark Vesey's insurrection in Charleston, South Carolina in 1822, Christian religion played a part in the plan. One message to his followers used Jesus' words "He that is not with me is against me" (Luke, 11:23).[40] Vesey's conspiracy also included an individual named Gullah Jack who used charms made from crab's claws to guarantee safety and victory to recruits.[41] Although the Vesey plot included both European and African religious influences, the possible flaw in this plot may have been that enlistees were restricted to artisans and freemen and therefore lacked numbers and force.[42]

In the Nat Turner rebellion, which took place in Southampton County, Virginia in 1831, Turner employed religion and mysticism. On February 12, Turner interpreted a solar eclipse as a sign from God. Within twenty-four hours, seventy slaves took part killing at least fifty-seven whites over a twenty-mile area. U.S. troops ended the uprising in a massacre of the slaves.[43]

From what is known, the drum was not used in the four revolts discussed above, but African-based cultural practices did have an impact on these actions. It can be argued that the more African the conspiracy, that is, the more the action involved African-based culture and religion, the greater the chances were for its success. Gabriel Prosser and Denmark

Vesey's rebellions have the legacy of being the least defined in terms of the conspirators' message and intentions. The conspiracies were both the efforts of assimilated blacks who included Christianity, and in Prosser's case, politics, in their message. In contrast, the Haitian revolution and the Nat Turner revolt were based on direct and brutal actions which clearly proposed the destruction of the white oppressor in their purpose.[44] Although the Turner revolt enlisted Christianity, and the Vesey plot included a conjurer, the number of assimilated participants was higher in the Prosser and Vesey plots. This implies a link between culture and action in that the Haitian and Turner revolts focused more on the continuance of African ways as a cause, whereas the Prosser and Vesey conspiracies sought a more complex political redress of the conditions of slavery. As a further example of the possible symbolism involved, Gabriel's revolt was inspired by the Old Testament emancipation of the ancient Israelites from Egypt,[45] and Denmark Vesey's plot began on Bastille Day.[46] These are the visions of an assimilated group.

I suggest in this brief assessment that the assimilation of African Americans served to both distance them from African culture, in ways beyond dance and music, and pull them into the ideological and political issues of American culture at that time. For such efforts African culture and the drum was simply no longer needed.

## Clandestine Activities

This chapter has so far presented documentary accounts that describe the use of the drum in revolts (Stono), the considerable fear of rebellions where drums or other tools of communication could be used (Georgia, Barbados), and the laws against such use. There are a number of descriptions that show continued prohibitions against the drum's use in the Caribbean and the United States and evidence of concessions to the cultural practices of slaves in North America (New Orleans), contrary to what might be thought of as being the case. By the early nineteenth century there is evidence of an acculturation process taking place in black American culture (Barclay, de la Beche), yet throughout the nineteenth century there are examples of continued opposition to the use of the drum (Mason, Police Jury) which in itself speaks to the drum's continuance.

These accounts have not told the whole story. Most of the descriptions portray public activities and talk about festivals or celebrations sanctioned by slaveholders. What is missing here are the clandestine activities of slaves and the activities which must have taken place away from the master's gaze. Was the fact that the drum was loud, and that its sound carried, prohibitive of nighttime events? Although this is a difficult question to answer, and this writer knows of no specific accounts of clandestine drumming, there is evidence of other clandestine slave activities. The following four reports illustrate the nature of secret religious meetings held by slaves in North America and some of the techniques used to avoid discovery.

In the 1843 autobiography of former slave Moses Grandy, he relates how after the Nat Turner rebellion religious meetings were suppressed. He also writes about prayer meetings held in the woods.[47] Black writer Octavia Victoria Rogers Albert describes in her 1891 work *The House of Bondage* how secret prayer meetings were held in cabins. In order to muffle the singing of hymns, a washtub full of water was put in the middle of the floor.[48] Other testimonies exist in the interviews of John B. Cade, a black professor whose article "Out of the Mouths of Ex-Slaves" appeared in the *Journal of Negro History* in 1935. His informants talk about secret prayer meetings in brush arbors. They also describe the use of pots turned upside down to muffle sounds. Others mention the use of quilts hung around worshipers to keep from discovery.[49] One final biography by Miles Mark Fisher titled *The Master's Slave*, published in 1922, describes the life of the author's father Elijah, who was a slave owner. In this work there is also mention of brush arbor services.[50] These testimonies give us a glimpse at the secret world of the slave and the measures taken to keep from discovery. Although these accounts do not talk about the drum directly, they do speak to the clandestine cultural practices under which drumming may have been carried out.

So far, the accounts referred to in this chapter, from 1654 (Desalles) to 1884 (Raum), have been described by whites about black activities. "Black codes" were instated after rebellions took place, further restrictions were put in place because of the fear of possible threats and some accounts, such as Le Page du Pratz's, appear to have been speculative. Moving away from the specter of what could have been, there is considerable testimony about what blacks in the early Americas did use the drum for that was not directly related to communication for rebellion. Festive dance or the appearance of celebration was not always the precursor for war, as the following accounts will attest to. What is more, slaves themselves make this clear.

## Communication

Slaves were known for communication techniques aside from the use of the drum. The use of signals and songs to assist runaway slaves was a common practice. It has been popularly known that such songs of movement, transference, and transcendence as "Swing Low, Sweet Chariot" were ripe with meaning.[51] This phenomenon was discussed in print not long after the end of slavery. In *Zion's Herald* for September 16, 1875, from Wentworth, North Carolina, there appeared an article called "Slave Telegraphy" that described signals used to alert slaves of oncoming patrollers.[52] In 1896 a *New England Magazine* article titled "Harriet Tubman" talked about the use of songs as signals to alert slaves.[53] Also in a *Colored American Magazine* article called "Famous Women of the Negro Race: Harriet Tubman ('Moses')," "alerting songs" are described as they were used in the Underground Railroad.[54]

The role of the drum in the day-to-day lives of slaves is revealed in the narratives of slaves themselves. The Slave Narrative Collection, gathered in the late 1930s from interviews with former slaves, is a source for such insights.[55] In particular the accounts of slaves from the Georgia Sea Islands, an area off the mainland coast of North America, has been a repository of continued African-based practices and beliefs. In contrast to the second-hand revelations of whites who viewed music and dance performance, these informants provide first-hand accounts. The interviews are both revealing and personal. Here the interviewers were white, and some scholars have had reservations regarding the limits this arrangement may have placed on the interviews.[56] Accepting this point, the narratives remain important due to the corroboration of practices and events that are given in varied ways by these surviving elderly African Americans.[57]

There are a number of examples of the use of the drum in communication. Josephine Stephens of Harris Neck, "a remote little settlement connected to the mainland by a causeway and located about forty-eight miles south of Savannah,"[58] was one of the older residents of the island. She was about 77 years old. The interviewer described Josephine and her daughter.

> As we talked with Josephine, the daughter stood in an adjoining room, ironing clothes. She stopped every now and then to take part in the conversation. The two women were utterly different types. Josephine, dressed becomingly in a blue and white checked gingham outfit, was the antebellum type of Negro. The daughter, tall, thin and dashing, and probably in her forties, represented a more modern era. She had on a blue checked sport shirt, a white skirt upon the surface of which was the dim outline of the trade name of a flour mill, and a pair of shiny black satin bedroom slippers. Her two front teeth were gold and shone and sparkled as she talked. Two large gold hoop earrings dangled beneath her close cropped straightened hair. . . .
>
> The mother did not know exactly how old she was but said she had been about fourteen at the close of the War between the States. . . .
>
> When we inquired about the drums being beaten at funerals, she shook her head stubbornly and refused to say anything on the subject.
>
> The daughter, overhearing the conversation, paused in her task of ironing, and said, "Yes'm. Dasso. . . . I remembuh heahin bout in the ole days they beat out messages on the drum. Let the folks know wen

> sumpm wuz bout tuh happen. Wen they give a dance ovuh on St. Catherine, they beat the drum tuh let the folks heah know bout it."[59]

The observations of the interviewer are interesting here, particularly the detailed descriptions of how the mother and daughter were dressed and how the mother was "antebellum" and the daughter "modern." The contrast is made more obvious by the fact that the mother refused to discuss drums at funerals while the daughter was forthcoming with that and more thoughts on the subject.

Susan Maxwell, a resident of Possum Point, talked about the death of her mother.

> She die right in dis house. Dey measure uh wid a string. Dey beat duh drum tuh tell ebrybody bout duh settin up. We all set up wid duh body. We hab a big wash pot full uh coffee and hab a big sack uh soda crackuh fuh duh folks. Ebrybody place dey han bery light on uh eahs an on uh nose an den dey say, "Dohn call me. I ain ready fuh tuh go yit."

Later, Susan mentioned how "In duh ole days dey beat duh drum tuh call duh people tuh duh fewnul."[60]

In his interview, Jack Tattnall, of Wilmington Island, talks similarly about the drum. "Wen a pusson die, we beat duh drum tuh let ebrybody know bout duh det. Den dey come tuh duh wake an sit up wid duh body."[61] Also Sophi Davis of White Bluff stated that "Yes'm dey alluz use tuh beat duh drum wen somebody die tuh let duh udduh folks know bout duh det."[62]

Issac Basden of Harris Neck was a blind basket maker who was about sixty years old. He described the drum's use. "I recall wen dey beat duh drum tuh call duh people on Harris Neck tuhgedduh fuh a dance aw fewnul."[63] Rachel Anderson of Possum Point also mentioned the use of the drum at funerals. "Right attuh duh pusson die, dey beat um tuh tell duh udduhs bout duh fewnul. . . . Dey beat duh drum in duh nex settlement tuh let duh folks in duh nex place heah."[64] Lawrence Baker, of Ridge road near Darien, discussed the drum. "Dey use tuh alluz beat duh drum aw blow duh hawn wen somebody die."[65] Rosa Sallins of Harris Neck also spoke of the drum's use to communicate.

> Yes'm, I membuh bout how some time back dey use tuh beat out messages on duh drum. Dat wuz tuh let us know wen deah wuz tuh be a dance aw a frolic. Wen dey hab a dance obuh on St. Catherines, dey beat duh drum tuh tell us bout it. Duh soun would carry obuh duh watuh an we would heah it plain as anyting. Den duh folks heah beat duh drum tuh let em know bout it in udduh settlements.[66]

Rosa's use of the word "message" suggests a kind of specificity to what was heard on the drum.

In an area called Baker's Crossing lived Ophelia Baker, who was a fortune teller and clairvoyant and was known by the name Madam Truth. She talked about the drum.

The plump, dark-skinned fortune teller said that she had spent her childhood on Skidaway Island. She remembered hearing the drums beaten to tell the people in the nearby settlements of an approaching dance or festival. Her father had been one of those who beat the drum and thumped out a regular message on it, a message that could be heard for miles and was clearly understood by all those who had heard it.[67]

Another woman, who was sitting on the front porch of her house, answered questions and talked about St. Catherine Island. The interviewer asked, "How would you know when they were going to hold a dance?" "Dey beat duh drums on St. Catherine. Den dey heah it at Harris Neck an folks deah tell all ub us yuh bout duh dance. We all go obuh tuh St. Catherine in a boat an dance an dance till mos daylight."[68]

This array of accounts shows how the drum was used in a very practical sense for communication. People were called together for dances by the drum. The drum was used as a form of advertisement from one island area to another of a coming event on that day or evening. The drum was also used to inform the community, in a telegraphic sense, of the death of a person. In addition to the use of the drum for the communication of a death, the following accounts talk about the use of the drum at funeral ceremonies. The residents also describe the types of drum rhythms that had specific meanings.

Jack Tattnall talked about funerals. "We beat duh drum agen at duh fewhul. . . . We call it duh dead mahch. Jis a long slow beat. Boom-boom-boom. Beat duh drum. Den stop. Den beat it agen. . . . At duh fewnul when we beat duh drum we mahch roun duh grabe in a ring."[69] Sophi Davis, in her interview, also added "An at fuwnuls too, dey beat it."[70]

Susan Maxwell gave other details of the funeral ceremony. "We bury uh by tawch light attuh dehk. Ebrybody mahch roun duh grabe in a succle. Ebry night attuh fewnul I put food on duh poach fuh duh spirit tuh come get it." She also described more specifically the way in which the drums beat at a funeral. "Dey beat it slow-boom-boom-boom. Wen dey wannuh stuhrup duh folks fuh a dance aw frolic, dey beats duh drum fas. Den dey knows it ain fuh no fewnul and dat it's fuh a good time."[71]

Josephine Stephen's daughter talked about funeral drums. "They beats the drum tuhday at the fewnul. Specially ef yuh blongs tuh a awganization, they goes right along in the fewnul pruhcession and beats the drum as they mahch."[72] Isaac Basden mentioned the types of beats the drum played for different occasions. "Case, dey hab a diffunt beat wen dey call um tuh a settin up aw fewnul frum duh one dey use tuh call um tuh a dance."[73] Rachel Anderson similarly described the type of drumming, "Use tuh alluz beat duh drum at fewnuls. . . . Dey beat a long beat. Den dey stop. Den dey beat anudduh long beat. Ebrybody know dat dis mean somebody die."[74]

Lawrence Baker also discussed the use of drums at funerals. "Dey beat two licks on duh drum, den dey stop, den dey beat tree licks. Wen yuh beat dat, uh know somebody done die. . . . Duh big drum wuz duh one dey beat at duh wake."[75] Rosa Sallins and Anna Johnson of Harris Neck mentioned the use of drums at funerals. They said that drums were played in the procession that accompanied the body to the grave.[76]

For these island residents the drum did talk and conveyed different meanings for different occasions. Here individuals have also articulated the different specific types of beats or rhythms they heard and what those rhythms meant to them. These reflections hint at the level of communication for which the drum was used in African American, and, earlier, African culture. One informant, Priscilla McCullough, who lived near Darien, touched on the relation between the drum and the individual within the community, and, in substitution for the drum in the new world, the banjo, as a voice of reconnoiter or justice for the group against the individual who had gone astray.

> Priscilla adjusted her eyeglasses which were tied on with a shoestring and told us something of the early life. She said she had been "bawn tree yeahs fo freedom in Sumtuh, Sout Calina," As quite a young woman she moved to Georgia but still retained many pleasant recollections of the days of her early youth. She had heard of many African customs and went on to tell us some of these.
>
> "I heard many time bout how in Africa wen a girl dohn cek jis lak dey should, day drum uh out uh town. Dey jis beat duh drum, an call uh name on duh drum and duh drum say bout all duh tings she done. Dey drum an meheh long a take duh girl right out uh town."
>
> "Girls hab tuh be keahful den. Dey cahn be so triflin lak some ub em is now. In Africa dey get punished. Sometime wen dey bin bad, dey put um on duh banjo. Dat wus in dis country."
>
> This being "put on duh banjo" was unintelligible to us and we asked for an explanation.
>
> "Wen dey play dat night, dey sing bout dat girl an dey tell all bout uh. Das putting uh on duh banjo. Den ebrybody know an dat girl sho bettuh chang eu ways."[77]

Priscilla first speaks to stories she heard about Africa as a girl as if these were abandoned practices. But when she explains being put on the banjo, it becomes clear that the banjo and voice has been substituted for the drum in America, and that a person's name is literally called out to the accompaniment of a banjo instead of being called out on a drum. A number of the residents talked about dancing to the drum. The woman sitting on her porch talks about dance. "We use tuh dance all duh time tuh duh drums," she said. "We would dance roun an roun in a sircle an clap our hans an sing. Dey would hab duh dances obuh on St. Catherine Ilun."[78] "I use to dance tuh duh drum," said Isaac Basden in his recollections.[79] Lawrence Baker recalled that, "Dey use drums at dances an meetins, to."[80]

There are also a number of accounts given of what the drums used to in fact look like. Robert Pickney gives one description. "Duh ole drums nut duh Africans make wuz make out ub a skin uh some kine uh animal stretch obuh a holluh lawg. Dey didn eben take duh haiah off duh skin. Jis put it on datta way."[81] Jack Tattnall talks about drum making. "Ain so long sence dey step makin drums. Wen I wuz a young man, we use tuh make um. Dey wuz fo cawhuhed sometimes an wuz cubbuh wid a skin. Dey wuz bout fo feet high."[82] Susan Maxwell remembered the types of drums used. "I kin membuh the kine uh drum, deah wuz duh lill kittle drum. Hit wuz bout fifteen inches cross an tree an a half foot high. Dat wuz duh drum dey beat fuh a settin up."[83] Isaac Basden also talked about drum types.

> Deah wuz two kine uh drum. One day call duh kittle drum, an one wuz duh bass drum. It stan bout two an a half foot high. Dey use tuh alluz hab a settin up wen somebody die. Wen folks would go tuh duh settin up, day would gib um bread an coffee.[84]

Lawrence Baker described a family of drums, three in number, that sound very much like drums used in Africa in size, and by the fact that goat skin was used to make the drum heads.[85]

> Lots uh duh drums wuz home made. Dey wuz made out uh goat skin an coon skin wut stretch out obuh heeps. Deah wuz tree sizes uh drums. Deah wuz duh big barrel drum. It wuz highuhn it wuz cross. Den deah wuz a lill drum frum twelve tuh fifteen inches wide an bout eighteen inches high. Duh udduh drum wuz duh medium size, kin euh in between duh udduh two. Duh big drum wuz duh one dey beat at duh wake. Dey use drums at dances an meetins, to.[86]

What is most significant about the drum descriptions is that these recollections place drum performances in the United States to the mid- to late-nineteenth century. These accounts come from a remote coastal island area of Georgia and not the mainland states. These interviews show that the African drum was used in this region of North America. This reality suggests that similar practices may have been possible in other areas of the South.

In the face of such forces native African drum and rhythmic practices might also be expected to adapt or somehow be absorbed in the acculturative process. As the drum came into disuse what took the place, in a culture for which this was an essential instrument? In fact black Americans found a multitude of ways in which to reassign or redistribute the function of the drum in music and dance. The next chapter will examine what surrogates were used in place of the drum.

## Background

For me the story of the African drum's use in America began with *The Slave Community* by John Blassingame (1945).[87] It was in this book that I first read about slaves "beating a drum as they marched," in the Stono Rebellion of 1739, and my interest in this subject was born. Blassingame was also the first author I read who described a complete black culture that existed with little relation to African Americans' status as slaves.

> Among the elements of slave culture were: an emotional religion, folk songs and tales, dances, and superstitions. Much of the slave's culture—language, customs, beliefs, and ceremonies—set him apart from his master.[88]

I was intrigued by the idea that there was an entire belief system, based on an African past, that the master class was not privy to. I was later exposed to other works that portray the wholeness and complexity of slave era African American culture. *Flash of the Spirit* by Robert Farris Thompson (1983)[89] and *Black Culture and Black Consciousness: Afro-American Folk Thought from Slavery to Freedom* by Lawrence Levine (1977), are among those.[90] Thompson, a scholar of African Art, focused his gaze on African American textiles, sculpture, iron works, and constructions for religious purposes, and identified unmistakable African-based design intentions. His perceptions and findings have had such focus as to allow him to regionalize certain artistic practices by African cultural groups in North America.[91] The strength of Levine's work is that he has tapped the oral traditions of storytelling, particularly heroic and animal tales, to show the rich oral literature that slaves created and passed on to later generations. Blassingame's earlier work did not martial such provocative evidence, but he remains for me the historian who best gave meaning to the idea of an independent black culture.

Blassingame makes other important points in the discussion of an original African American culture. He found that Africans' "link with their past" was itself a form of resistance to bondage.[92] He delineates, in terms of music, what actual instruments came into use. "Drums, guitars, flutes, piccolos, whistles and horns were the principal instruments and were played on many occasions."[93] To support the concept that African American practices were foreign to Europeans, Blassingame quotes one Englishman on African dance. "The body movements are extremely difficult and would probably kill a European."[94] Through such presentations the author suggested a form to African American culture, and that slave activities were not necessarily understood or appreciated.

The single most important source of documentary accounts of black music and dance in the New World is *Sinful Tunes and Spirituals* by Dena Epstein (1977).[95] This documentary colossus, written by a librarian, was over ten years in the making and was supported by grants from the National Endowment and the Andrew W. Mellon Foundation. The actual focus of this book is the development of the spiritual and how this vocal form was discovered and recorded by interested Northern whites, some of whom were active abolitionists, in the mid- to late-nineteenth century. At least the first half of this four-hundred-and-fifteen-page book, which includes notated musical examples, is devoted to the presentation of excerpts from travel journals and diaries of black American performance as witnessed by Europeans and Americans. Epstein treats all of the African American performing arts, music, dance, and song and organizes the material chronologically by region and topic.

Epstein describes a number of impressions about the prohibition of the drum as well as its possible continuance. She in fact asks some of the same questions regarding the documentary evidence that I have faced in the present work, and I have learned from her observations. For example, in one discussion early in the book the author concludes that such "African dancing in the backwoods would be repressed by the growing settlement of the area."[96] Epstein also mentions a discrepancy in the accounts of black performance, different from but not unlike my own queries. "The apparent contradiction between the miseries of slavery and such vigorous dancing and singing created great problems in the thinking of Europeans and their American descendants."[97] In a similar way she addresses, in an almost frustrated tone, the problems of using disparate historical accounts.

These fragmentary accounts from the early eighteenth century tell little more than that Africans danced in a manner that was considered heathenish in South Carolina, New York, the Leeward Islands, Maryland, Virginia, and North Carolina.[98]

Epstein was not able to utilize the Slave Narrative Collection in her work but does state that "it undoubtedly includes much valuable material."[99]

Epstein's opinions fall within what I have termed the revisionist view that the "mainland colonies, with the exception of Louisiana, found it possible strictly to enforce the regulations, judging from the relative absence of drums and drumming in accounts from the mainland."[100] I question this conclusion and have used the known occurrence of clandestine activities as well as the use of communicating signals and songs to set up a larger discussion of accounts that shows the use of the drum as a tool for communication in nonviolent ways in the Georgia Sea Islands. In spite of her conclusion that the regulation of drumming was "strictly" enforced, Epstein contradicts her own assessment elsewhere in the text. "Yet African drumming must have continued surreptitiously in the United States, since interviews collected by the Federal Writers' Project in the 1930's describe it vividly."[101]

The present study accomplishes what historical anthologies such as Epstein's could not. I have focused on one topic within the broad spectrum of the African American performance arts and have drawn that idea through the eras of American history. This project has also taken on the point of view that in spite of everything, African drumming never ceased, and has turned to documentary findings to see if a case can be made for that thesis. Where documentary histories tend to be chronologies or collections of materials, I have devised a question that can be tested using this documentary evidence. The nature of my topical study has allowed me to tap a wider array of sources than other works on black culture. I know of no other historical study that has utilized the resources of documentary anthologies described here. For example, Epstein in *Sinful Tunes* mentions that she did not search newspapers or magazines, while *African-American Traditions in Song, Sermon, Tale, and Dance, 1600s–1920* by Eileen Southern (1990) does source a variety of these materials from early America, but does not include the types of personal accounts from Europeans and Americans that *Sinful Tunes* and *Black Dance* utilize. There has also been a personal process involved here. I first saw quotations and images in books. I later in my own research sought out the archival originals to these resources to understand the whole, the greater context of a passage or item.

What is interesting about comparing the present thesis of a Sea Island model of drum continuance that might be applied to other areas of America is that *Slave Songs of the United States* published by William Francis Allen in 1867, the foremost collection of black spirituals, has for over a hundred years been the model for all of black song, and it was based on collecting efforts from the same region of the country. If the Gullah people can be a model for song, why not for the drum?[102]

Second to *Sinful Tunes*, the following three works have been equally important to this project in providing documentary accounts. First among those is *Black Dance in the United States from 1619 to 1970* by Lynne Emery (1972).[103] This book is primarily an assessment of the history and development of black dance. The amount and types of accounts presented make this book an important source. The early sections of the book are much like *Sinful Tunes* in terms of presentation but the excerpts focus more specifically on dance descriptions. Emery also speaks to the drum's prohibition and comments on the continuance of African traditions in the face of slavery.

With the blacks, the drums and the calabash left Africa. Still the drumming sounded, but now with the metallic clank of overturned buckets and tubs on the ship decks. The drums, and those who played them, arrived in the New World, and the dances they accompanied reached the West Indies, where they continued much as they had in Africa. It was only as the drums and people reached the United States that the sound of Africa diminished. The drums were prohibited, and yet the rhythms of Africa lived on in new forms among the slaves as bare feet stomped on the hard earth, hands clapped, and songs were sung.[104]

Here Emery addresses a type of continuance of African traditions in dance, but again without the drum.

*African-American Traditions* places an emphasis on religion as the most important aspect of black American culture. She also acknowledges the central role of the drum.[105] "At the heart of their culture were their religions, which, encompassing the song, drum, and dance along with prayer, proverbs, and ceremonies, pervaded just about every phase of their lives, from birth to the grave."[106] In a manner similar to what I have tried to show for the drum, Southern finds a continuance of African ways that is coincident with the slave's adaptation to and change within their environment. She states that the writings of various observers "attest to the strength of African survivals among the slaves at a time when they were being assimilated into a new religious and social environment."[107] These early writers employed a variety of formats for their publications, most frequently the travelogue, but also diaries, journals, letters, regional and national histories, sermons, and political tracts. Additionally, runaway slave advertisements, broadsides, and other kinds of ephemeral publications provide sources of information about black culture.[108]

Southern also points out the special role, in terms of point of view, that African American voices have in the historical record. "The black narrator, like the white narrator, reported on religious rituals, recreational activities, and other features of plantation daily life, but seen from his perspective, these matters take on a different character."[109]

*Afro-American Folk Culture* by John F. Szwed (1978) is an earlier work than *Traditions* and reveals a totally different set of sources. One unique feature of this volume is the inclusion of foreign language research, most notably from Cuba is Fernando Ortiz's *Los Instrumentos de la Musica Afro-Cubana* (1952). All of the references that I found valuable were books, as opposed to the archival papers of an individual or periodical article. For example, *Shining Trumpets* by Rudi Blesh (1946), which includes descriptions of New Orleans culture in the late nineteenth century, is listed in the bibliography as NA248, referring to texts for North America.[110] I was encouraged by Szwed's own interest in the continuance of the African-based drum in North America, as demonstrated in the following passage. Included in the references he cites are *Drums and Shadows*, and the early American novel *Satanstoe* by James Fenimore Cooper.

> For those convinced that drums were completely forbidden under slavery in North America with the result that African drums and drumming were irretrievably lost there is the countertestimony of. . . . From Congo Square in New Orleans to upstate New York, from backwoods Louisiana to coastal Georgia, drums have been heard and remarked upon from the 1700's to the present. During Juneteenth celebrations—Emancipation Day—drums and drum dances are still important . . . and local oral history traces the custom to slavery times.

Overall, this bibliography is made up of "published works on Afro-American folk culture, thus excluding dissertations, manuscripts and the like."[111] Szwed has divided the literature of black American folk culture into four phases. Travel accounts and journal entries from the seventeenth and eighteenth centuries make up the first phase. A second phase begins with the writings, in the early nineteenth century, of abolitionists who concerned themselves with questions of emancipation and the Christianity of the slave. The third phase includes post slavery writings of former slaveholders, a literature of reflection on the former slave state. The fourth phase, beginning in the 1930s, analyzes black culture as different from the mainstream.[112]

*Slave Testimony* by John Blassingame (1977) is a large seven hundred and forty-five-page collection of narratives and interviews from published books, newspapers, and magazines and the Slave Narrative Collection. Blassingame is the most critical historian regarding the usefulness and validity of the Slave Narrative Collection. In his introduction, the author first points out that because of the long life spans of the Collection informants, they cannot be considered typical slaves.[113] There are other reasons for his reservations.

Taken at face value, there seems to have been a bias in many states toward including the most obsequious former slaves. This is especially true when most of the informants had spent all their lives in the same locale as their former master's plantation. Since the least satisfied and most adventuresome of the freed slaves might have migrated to Northern states or to cities after the Civil War, the WPA informants may have been atypical of antebellum slaves.[114]

Blassingame goes on to point out that "in spite of the skewed sample," the Collection "reveals much about the nature of slavery" and "contain[s] a large repository of folklore."[115] He mentions that in the Collection there are "probably more religious and secular songs than any other single collection" and that such works, used with published slave narratives, "will enable historians to write more revealing and accurate portrayals of slavery."[116] Blassingame also speaks to the need for researchers to utilize a variety of types of evidence, and writes about interviews versus published individual slave narratives as being complementary to one another. "The interviews include the women (fifty percent of the total) and 'average' slaves who did not publish their stories; the narratives include the blacks from the border states missing in the interviews."[117] He makes an additional point that in "antebellum newspapers, magazines, and books" there appeared hundreds of accounts of slaves that historians could utilize in addition to narratives and the interviews in the Collection.

In this massive text there is only one interview that mentions the use of the drum, and this was by a slave who was a drummer during the Civil War. I have not been able to account for the fact that this text has so few references to culture. There are only three references to music and musicians and two accounts that mention communication. This is the same author who, in *The Slave Community*, set the tone for research into the culture of the African American. I think that it is only a matter of editorial choice and an interest in the portrayal of lifestyle and life history in *Slave Testimony* that can account for this difference.[118]

*Music in New Orleans. The Formative Years 1791–1841* by Henry Kmen (1966) provided the insights into African American performance practices in the South that led to my suggestion that the paradigm of severe restrictions on musical performance was not necessarily the case. Kmen offers up six different accounts of the use of the drum in mostly acculturated situations. His book chronicles the interest in dance and march music among the upper classes and the common people of New Orleans during the National period of American history. In a discussion of the white society balls of New Orleans, Kmen states that:

> The women might be too fatigued for fireworks, but they were willing to walk barefoot through two miles of mud to get to a dance in the days before New Orleans had sidewalks. After a footbath at the door and a change into the costumes carried by their slaves, they were ready to dance for seven hours and then to brave the mud again on the journey home.[119]

The one account of African styled drumming addresses a different national music.

> They have their own national music, consisting for the most part of a long kind of narrow drum of various sizes, from two to eight feet in length, three or four of which make a band. The principal dancers or leaders are dressed in a variety of wild and savage fashions, always ornamented with a number of the tails of the smaller wild beasts.[120]

This description by Christian Schultz, a traveler, from his book of 1810 makes clear that the African ways were still present. An account from another traveler is among a few which describe fife and drum performances. Henry Didimus, during his stay in New Orleans, mentions being awakened by "negroes" early on a Sunday in 1835 "in full regimentals" playing "Yankee Doodle" on fife and drum.[121]

This consideration of historiography relevant to the prohibition of the drum will now jump in time to our own age to present two final ideas on the drum as symbol in American culture.

*Time* magazine's June 12, 1995 issue included a "forum" titled "Tough Talk on Entertainment" where nine writers, artists, and politicians wrote brief commentaries on Republican Congressman Robert Dole's attack on Hollywood and the need for self-censorship. African American author John Edgar Wideman contributed to this piece. Describing the controversy over the harshness of current movies and of rap music, the author remarks:

> I wasn't around when black people were barred from playing drums. But I know the objections to African drumming weren't aesthetic; southern legislators feared the drums' power to signal a general slave revolt. I was around when finding black music on the radio was a problem. Growing up in Pittsburgh, Pennsylvania, the only way to hear the latest rhythm-and-blues sounds after dark was searching the scratchy hyperspace for Randy's Record Shack beaming up from Nashville, Tennessee. Banning, ignoring, exploiting, damning black art has a long history. Protecting black freedom of expression and participation at all levels of society began just yesterday. . . .

Wideman's final point is that America must not fear art that challenges tradition. "The best art interrogates and explodes consensus."[122]

In 1990, a more than sixty-year-old ban on drums and horns was overturned for establishments defined as a "cabaret."[123] Paul Chevigny in his book *Gigs: Jazz and the Cabaret Laws in New York City* (1991) states "live music played in bars and restaurants in New York City was restricted by local regulations called collectively 'the cabaret laws.'" The laws "not only forbade percussion as well as typical jazz front-line instruments such as horns, but it restricted the number of musicians to three." "On January 28th, 1988, Justice Saxe declared the entire 'incidental musical entertainment' exception unconstitutional."[124] It appears that the ban on drums and horns in Barbados in 1699, St. Kitts in 1711 and 1722, Jamaica in 1717, and South Carolina and Georgia following the Stono Rebellion of 1739, had, until recently, a late-twentieth-century equivalent. It is well known how the African American music known as jazz has always borne the brunt of a stigma of lasciviousness. The cabaret law shows a connection to the morals of our country that is as old as America itself.

## Notes

1 Sir Hans Sloane, *A Voyage to the Islands of Madera, Barbados, Nieces, S. Christopher and Jamaica, with the Natural History of the . . . Last of These Islands. . . .* (London: Printed by B. M. for the Author, 1707). This passage is cited in two places by Dena Epstein in *Sinful Tunes and Spirituals: Black Folk Music to the Civil War* (Chicago: University of Chicago Press, 1977), 29 and 58 and is also found in Lynne Emery, *Black Dance in the United States from 1619 to 1970* (Princeton, 1972), 18.

2 General Oglethorpe to the Accotant, Mr. Harman Verelst, October 9, 1739, in Allen D. Candler, comp., *The Colonial Records of the State of Georgia. . . .* (Atlanta: C. P. Byrd, 1913). See *Sinful Tunes* 39.

3 South Carolina, *Laws, Statutes, etc. The Statutes at Large of South Carolina*, ed. Thomas Cooper and David J. McCord (Columbia: Printed by A. S. Johnston, 1836–41). See *Sinful Tunes* 59.

4 Laws Georgia, *Statutes, etc. A Codification of the Statute Law of Georgia, Including the English Statutes of Force. . . . Compiled, digested and arranged, by William A. Hotchkiss, by Authority of the Legislature* (Savannah: J. M. Cooper, 1845). See *Sinful Tunes* 62.

5 Dena Epstein makes the point that the South Carolina law incorporated provisions of slave acts from the Caribbean. I have not located any earlier versions of this language.

6 See, Eugene D. Roll Genovese and Roll Jordan, *The World the Slaves Made* (New York, 1974), 594. These are the author's words. A similar description is in Harvey Wish, "American Slave Insurrections Before 1861," *The Journal of Negro History* 22 (July 1937) in John H. Bracey, Jr., ed., *American Slavery: The Question of Resistance* (CA: Belmont, 1971), 31. Wish describes a January 1811 revolt at Pointe Coupee, Louisiana. "Their force, estimated to include from 180 to 500 persons, was defeated in a pitched battle with the troops." "The Negroes formed disciplined companies to march upon New Orleans to the beating of drums." Because these descriptions are so similar, I have concluded that they must have been the same event.

7 Adrien Dessalles, *Histoire Generale des Antilles* (Paris, 1847–48). This is Epstein's translation of Dessalles. See *Sinful Tunes* 27.

8 Le Page du Pratz, *Histoire de la Louisianne* (Paris: De Bure l'aine, 1758). See *Sinful Tunes* 32.

9 See, Emery, *Black Dance* 18–24 for a discussion of the Calenda.

10 Jeffrey Brackett, *The Negro in Maryland* (Baltimore, 1889), 100. See *Sinful Tunes* 59.

11 An Abridgement of the Laws in Force and Use in Her Majesty's, *Plantations (Viz) of Virginia, Jamaica, Barbados, Maryland, New England, New York, Carolina, &c. Digested under Proper Heads in the Method of Mr. Wingate, and Mr. Washington's Abridgements* (London: J. Nicholson, 1704), 239. See *Sinful Tunes* 59.

12 South Carolina, Laws, Statutes, etc., Statutes at Large, VII (1840): 354, "An Act for the Better Ordering and Governing of Negroes and Slaves . . . ratified . . . the seventh day of June . . . 1712." See *Sinful Tunes* 59.

13 Elsa V Goveia, *Slave Society in the British Leeward Islands at the End of the Eighteenth Century*, (New Haven, 1965), 156. See *Sinful Tunes* 59.

14 Lawrence Henry Gipson, *The British Isles and the American Colonies: The Southern Plantations, 1748–1754* (New York: Knopf, 1960), 199. See *Sinful Tunes* 59.

15 Edward Marcus Despard, Esq. A Narrative of the Publick Transactions in the Bay of Honduras from 1784 to 1790. Public Record Office, Kew, Richmond, Surrey, England PRO reference: C.O. 123/10 (Colonial Office Records) 1791. 73–92. I would like to thank Cliff Connor for sharing this account from his research on Colonel Despard.

16 Sir William Young, "A Tour through the Several Islands of Barbadoes, St. Vincent, Antigua, Tobago, and Grenada, in the Years 1791 & 1792," in *Edwards, Bryan The History, Civil and Commercial, of the British West Indies* (London: Printed for J. Stockdale, 1793–1801), III, 261–301.

17 In 1712, New York was the place of another major rebellion carried out by slaves. Then, twenty-five slaves set fire to a building and killed nine whites.

18 James Howard Brewer, "Legislation Designed to Control Slavery in Wilmington and Fayetteville," *North Carolina Historical Review* 30 (April, 1953), 155–66. See *Sinful Tunes* 60.

19 In contrast to Dena Epstein, who shows both patterns of effective prohibition and the continuance of African based cultural practices, Eileen Southern finds that the acculturative transition was complete by the mid-eighteenth century and that "The favorite instrument for dance music was the violin, played by white and black fiddlers." See, Eileen Southern, *The Music of Black Americans* (New York, 1971), 26.

20 In *Sinful Tunes* 144, Dena Epstein finds that: "The omnipresent drums of the West Indies were not heard on the mainland—not even at slave dances, where other percussive devices (sticks, bones, tambourines, and clapping) had to take their place." This statement is taken from a discussion by the author describing the mid-eighteenth century.

21 Thomas Jefferys, *The Natural and Civil History of the French Dominions in North and South America. . . .* (London: Printed for T. Jefferys, 1760). See *Sinful Tunes* 31.

22 Jamaica. Laws, Statutes, etc. The New Act of Assembly of the Island of Jamaica . . . Commonly Called the New Consolidated Acts . . . Passed . . . the 6th Day of December, 1788; *Being the Present Code Noir of the Island.* Published by Stephen Fuller (London: Printed for B. White and Son, 1789). See *Sinful Tunes* 62.

23 Henry A. Kmen, *Music in New Orleans; the Formative Years, 1791–1841* (Baton Rouge, 1966).

24 Francois-Xavier Martin, *The History of Louisiana, from the Earliest Period. . . .* (New Orleans: Printed by Lyman and Beardslee, 1827). See *Sinful Tunes* 92.

25 New Orleans, *Ordinances, etc. Police Code, or Collection of the Ordinances of Police Made by the City Council of New Orleans. . . .* (New Orleans: Printed by J. Renard, 1808). See *Sinful Tunes* 93.

26 George Washington Cable has most famously written about the Congo Square celebrations in New Orleans that took place in the late nineteenth century. "The Dance in Place Congo," which describes African-based drumming and dance, appeared in *The Century Magazine* in 1886. See Bernard Katz, ed., *The Social Implications of Early Negro Music in the United States* (New York, 1969).

27 Dena Epstein describes acculturation in a more general sense, effecting music and dance, holidays and festivals in chapter four of *Sinful Tunes* 77–99.

28 H.T. De la Beche, *Notes on the Present Condition of the Negroes in Jamaica* (London: Printed for T. Cadell, 1825). See, *Sinful Tunes* 86. "Joncanoe" refers to the John Canoe festivals held throughout the Caribbean during Christmas. See Lynne Emery's remarks on the tradition in *Black Dance* 30–4.

29 Alexander Barclay, *A Practical View of the Present State of Slavery in the West Indies; or, An Examination of Mr. Stephen's "Slavery of the British West India Colonies:" Containing More Particularly an Account of the Actual Condition of the Negroes in Jamaica. . . .*, 3rd ed., with additions (London: Smith, Elder, 1828). See *Sinful Tunes* 86.

30 Mrs. A.C. Carmichael, *Domestic Manners and Social Conditions of the White, Coloured and Negro Population of the West Indies. . . .* (London: Whittaker, Treacher, 1833).

31 See *Black Dance* 48.

32 Edward G. Mason, "A Visit to South Carolina in 1860," *Atlantic Monthly* 53 (February 1884), 241–50. See *Sinful Tunes* 60.

33 "Code Noir; or, Black Code of Louisiana," *The Commercial Review of the South and West* 1 (May 1846), 410–11. later entitled De Bow's Review. See, Eileen Southern, *African-American Traditions in Song, Sermon, Tale, and Dance, 1600s–1920* (Westport, 1990). citation no. 81.

34 Minutes of the Police Jury, Aug. 13, 1849, MS, cited in Vernie Alton Moody, "Slavery on Louisiana Sugar Plantations," Reprinted from the Louisiana Historical Quarterly April, 1924. See *Sinful Tunes* 60.

35 Green Raum, *The Existing Conflict* (Washington, DC, 1884), 273–4. See, John F. Szwed, *Afro-American Folk Culture: An Annotated Bibliography of Materials from North, Central, and South America and the West Indies* (Philadelphia: Institute for the Study of Human Issues, 1978).

36 See *The Music* 69.

37 See, Eileen Southern, *Readings in Black American Music* (New York, 1971), 52.

38 See, C. L. R. James, *The Black Jacobins: Toussaint L'Ouverture and the San Domingo Revolution* (London, 1978).

39 See, Gerald W. Mullin, *Flight and Rebellion: Slave Resistance in Eighteenth-Century Virginia* (New York, 1972). Mullin finds that Gabriel's rebellion lacked "a sacred dimension, was without a Moses, and thus without a following." p. 160.

40 See, Eugene D. Genovese, *From Rebellion to Revolution: Afro-American Slave Revolts in the Making of the Modern World* (Baton Rouge, 1979), 10.

41 See, John Bracey, Jr., ed., *American Slavery; the Question of Resistance*, (CA, 1971), 147.

42 See, *Flight and Rebellion* 160. Understanding Denmark Vesey's revolt has led to controversy among historians. In Bracey's *American Slavery* a series of three articles take the respective points of view that (1) religion was an important aspect of the plot (Herbert Aptheker), (2) that the conspiracy may never have existed and may have been a fabrication (Richard C. Wade), and (3) that the plan was indeed extensive, and was inspired by both Old Testament ideology and intelligence on the revolution in Haiti. 120–47.

43 See, Herbert Aptheker, *American Negro Slave Revolts* (New York, 1943), 293–300.

44 Eugene Genovese also discusses eighteenth-century New York rebellions. "The New York rebels espoused traditional African religion, as they understood it, and called for a war on the Christians in a manner suggestive of the early Caribbean Obeahmen and foreshadowing the call to arms of the Vodun priests of Saint Domingue." See, *Rebellion to Revolution* 42.

45 See, Harvey Wish, "American Slave Insurrections before 1861," *The Journal of Negro History* 22 (July 1937) in *American Slavery* 27.

46 See *Rebellion to Revolution* 130.

47 Moses Grandy, *Narrative of the Life of Moses Grandy, Late a Slave of the United States of America*, ed. George Thompson (London: C. Gilpin, 1843), 45See Traditions citation no. 262.

48 Octavia Victoria Rogers Albert, *The House of Bondage; or, Charlotte Brooks and other Slaves* (New York: Hunt & Eaton, 1891), 161. See Traditions citation no. 707.

49 John B. Cade, "Out of the Mouths of Ex-Slaves," *Journal of Negro History* 20 (1935), 294–337. See Traditions citation no. 1865.

50 Miles Mark Fisher, *The Master's Slave: Elijah John Fisher: A Biography by His Son Miles Mark Fisher* (Philadelphia: Judson Press, 1922), 194. See Traditions citation no. 1942.

51 See Roger Thurman, *Deep River and the Negro Spiritual Speaks of Life and Death* (Richmond, 1975). Thurman concludes that Christian song served another practical function in that it allowed slaves "to reject annihilation and affirm a terrible right to live." p. 127.

52 N. C. Wentworth, "Slave Telegraphy," *Zion's Herald* 52 (16 September, 1875) [2891]. See Traditions citation no. 1398.

53 Lillie B. Chace Wyman, "Harriet Tubman," *New England Magazine* n.s. 14 (March 1896), 110–18. See Traditions citation no. 1404.

54 Pauline E. Hopkins, "Famous Women of the Negro Race: Harriet Tubman ('Moses')," *Colored American Magazine* 4 (January–February 1902), 210–23. See Traditions citation no. 2056.

55 See, Writers' Program, *Georgia: Drums and Shadows; Survival Studies among the Georgia Coastal Negroes [by the] Savannah Unit, Georgia Writers' Project, Work Projects Administration* (Athens, 1940).

56 Criticism of the Slave Narrative Collection is addressed in the historiography section which follows.

57 One important factor about the narratives is that they represent a specific time period or range of years. The individuals quoted in the present section are from sixty to ninety years old.

58 See, *Drums and Shadows* 113.

59 See, Ibid. 118.

60 See, Ibid. 135.
61 See, Ibid. 100.
62 See, Ibid. 71.
63 See, Ibid. 114.
64 See, Ibid. 133.
65 See, Ibid. 147.
66 See, Ibid. 122.
67 See, Ibid. 84.
68 See, Ibid. 111.
69 See, Ibid. 100.
70 See, Ibid. 71.
71 See, Ibid. 135.
72 See, Ibid. 118.
73 See, Ibid. 114.
74 See, Ibid. 132.
75 See, Ibid. 147.
76 See, Ibid. 120.
77 See, Ibid. 146.
78 See, Ibid. 110.
79 See, Ibid. 114.
80 See, Ibid. 147.
81 See, Ibid. 100.
82 See, Ibid.
83 See, Ibid. 135.
84 See, Ibid. 114.
85 See, J. H. Kwabena Nketia, *The Music of Africa* (New York, 1974), 85–91 for a discussion of African drum types and materials.
86 See, *Drums and Shadows* 147.
87 John Blassingame, *The Slave Community: Plantation Life in the Antebellum South* (New York, 1972).
88 Ibid. 41.
89 Robert Farris Thompson, *Flash of the Spirit* (New York, 1983).
90 Lawrence W. Levine, *Black Culture and Black Consciousness: Afro-American Folk Thought from Slavery to Freedom* (New York, 1977).
91 See also, Roger Bastide, *African Civilizations in the New World* (New York, 1971).
92 *Slave Community* 24.
93 Ibid. 19.
94 Ibid. 20.
95 See, Dena J. Epstein, *Sinful Tunes and Spirituals: Black Folk Music to the Civil War*. Urbana and Chicago: University of Illinois Press, 1977.
96 Ibid. 43.
97 Ibid. 42.
98 Ibid. 39.
99 Ibid. xvii.
100 Ibid. 60.
101 Ibid. 53.
102 See, *Traditions*.
103 See, *Black Dance*.
104 Ibid. 80.

105 See, *Traditions*.
106 See, Ibid. 21.
107 See, Ibid. 22.
108 See, Ibid. 22.
109 See, Ibid. 28.
110 See, *Folk Culture*.
111 See, Ibid. xiii.
112 See, Ibid. xi–xii.
113 See, *Slave Testimony*, ed. John Blassingame (Baton Rouge, 1977), li.
114 See, Ibid.
115 See, Ibid. lv.
116 See, Ibid. lvi.
117 See, Ibid.
118 See, Ibid. 284. William Houston was interviewed in 1852, approximately. He was forty-two years old and was born in 1810 in Gibraltar and enslaved in Louisiana.
119 See, *New Orleans* 5.
120 From Schultz, *Christian Travels on an Inland Voyage . . . in the Years 1807 and 1808*, 2 vols (New York, 1810). See, *New Orleans* 227.
121 From Didimus, *Henry New Orleans as I Found It* (New York, 1845), 36. See, *New Orleans* 202.
122 See, "Tough Talk on Entertainment," *Time* (June 12, 1995), 32–35.
123 The New York City cabaret licensing ordinance defines a cabaret as any "room place or space in the city in which any musical entertainment . . . is permitted . . . which provide incidental musical entertainment . . . by not more than three persons playing piano, organ, acordian [sic], guitar or any stringed instrument." See, Paul Chevigny, *Gigs: Jazz and the Cabaret Laws in New York City* (New York, 1991).
124 See, *Gigs* 1, 15 and 127.

# 4 Surrogates

## Juba, Shouts & Rhythm

Beginning with the premise that humans are ultimately adaptable, it is natural that the response to cultural suppression among African Americans might be the creation of something new. For the various reasons that the African drum was banned or not, other rhythmic practices were both continued and created. African music has always had, as part of its character, the use of many other rhythmic devices in addition to the drum.[1] The African American musical experience is perhaps unique in that rhythmic traditions flourished here in the face of the great restriction on drum playing.[2] The literature of third party accounts, slave narratives, and interviews speaks to the variety of manifestations of a metric aesthetic in black American performance. These practices represented surrogates for the often-missing drum.

Set in this context, many common folk musical practices take on a unique light. To start, the Slave Narrative Collection can provide examples.[3] There are, for instance, accounts by former slaves of the use of everyday objects such as wash tubs, kettles, buckets, tin cans, skillets, pieces of steel, bones, bottles, wooden sticks and broom straws that were used as musical instruments to provide rhythm. The practice of "patting juba" was also mentioned, a type of rhythmic accompaniment performed by an individual clapping and patting their legs, arms, and torso. Horns are described that were used as a form of communication to awaken slaves before dawn, summon slaves from the fields and as a signal for slave gatherings (in one case "the horn was over a foot long and kept polished so that it shone"[4]). Manufactured instruments such as the violin and tambourine, as well as homemade versions of the same, were also in use. Straws "used to beat on the fiddles" and "knocking two bones behind the fiddle" were commonly described ways of rhythmic accompaniment. In addition to these varied accounts, and with much less frequency, are remembrances of "folk crafted," "cow-hide," and "homemade" drums by those interviewed.

As a further example, John Cole of Georgia, formerly a slave on the Oglethorpe plantation, recounts the use of various instruments. "Stretch cow-hides over cheeseboxes and you had tambourines. Saw bones from off a cow, knock them together, and call it a drum, or use broom-straws on fiddle-strings, and you had your entire orchestra."[5] Here are substitutes for not only the manufactured tambourine, but for the rhythms of the drum.

This chapter will present the alternative performance practices to the playing of the drum as carried out by slaves. Juba, the shout (a religious ring dance), horns, bells, and string instruments will each be considered in turn, in order to show (1) their function as musical performance, (2) the surrogate role to the drum of the instrument or practice for African Americans, and (3) their part in the creativity of black culture. This analysis will be followed by a critical consideration of what other historians have described.

## Drumless Drummers

In a literal sense African Americans continued to drum without the drum. A half-dozen various accounts beginning in the mid-nineteenth century and ending in the 1930s portray drumming using sticks on various surfaces.[6] In 1836 a slave fiddler was described in *The Southern Rose*, a magazine for children. "Diggony" was accompanied by "a tall, stout, fellow beating a triangle, and another drumming with two long sticks on a piece of weed."[7] On March 29, 1843, William Cullen Bryant witnessed a dance in Barnwell District, South Carolina, where blacks made music by "whistling, and beating time with the sticks upon the floor."[8] A recollection of Elizabeth Cexe of a plantation in South Carolina during the Civil War included this comment. "Every day of Christmas week, in the afternoon, the negroes dance in the broad piazza until late at night, the orchestra consisting of two fiddlers, one man with bones, and another had sticks with which he kept time on the floor, and sometimes singing."[9] James Bolton of Oglethorpe County, Georgia, mentions a recollection of music playing from the late nineteenth century. "After supper we used to gather around and knock tin buckets and pans. We beat them like drums. Some used their fingers, and some used sticks for to make the drum sounds and most always somebody blowed on quills."[10] The use of sticks on other surfaces to accompany drums is also a commonly described practice. In 1816, Matthew Lewis described a celebration of his slaves in Cornwall, Jamaica. "The music consisted of nothing but Gambys (Eboe drums), Shaky-shekies, and Kitty-katties; the latter is nothing but any flat piece of board beat upon with two sticks, and the former is a bladder with a parcel of pebbles in it."[11]

Alcee Fortier's "Customs and Superstitions in Louisiana" that appeared in the *Journal of American Folklore* for July 1888 details the use of stick accompaniment as well as some of the author's opinions on the music.

> The principal musician bestrode the barrel and began to beat on the hide, singing as loud as he could. He beat with his hands, with his feet,

> and sometimes, when quite carried away by his enthusiasm, with his head also. The second musician took the sticks and beat on the wood of the barrel, while the third made a dreadful music by rattling the teeth of the jawbone with a stick. Five or six men stood around the musicians and sang without stopping. . . . These dancing-songs generally consisted of one phrase, repeated for hours on the same air.[12]

In spite of the questionable observation that the drummer drummed with his feet and head, and the apparently "dreadful music," this late-nineteenth-century observation is worthy of note because of the obvious unacculturated practices of the participants. Most important is the reference to a chorus involved in call and response or a phrase repetition with the drumming. Aurally, or acoustically, this is a basic and interesting ensemble comprised of the sounds of membrane, wood, and rattle. In his accounts of the music and dance of Congo Square in New Orleans, George Washington Cable also writes about sticks on drums.

> the drums were laid along on the turf and the drummers bestrode them, and beat them on the head madly with fingers, fists, and feet,—with slow vehemence on the great drum, and fiercely and rapidly on the small one. Sometimes an extra performer sat on the ground behind the larger drum, at its open end, and "beat upon the wooden sides of it with two sticks."[13]

As mentioned in Chapter Two, Cable's flamboyant language has raised questions regarding the objectivity of his reports. Here a drummer also plays with his "feet." From Elizabeth W. Allston Pringle's *A Woman Rice Planter* is the memory of Christmas celebrations of slaves that were made up of the music of fiddle, tambourine, bones, drum, and sticks.[14] These accounts suggest two conclusions, first, that rhythmic practices accompanying the drum continued as they had existed before in Africa, and, second, that stick drumming continued even though the drum was a banned instrument.

## Juba

Juba is the much-described rhythmic practice of African Americans that has also been referred to as a dance, a song, a person (Master Juba), and a state of being. This section will present slave narratives that mention juba performance, detailed third party accounts of how juba was done, more general references to juba as accompaniment for dance, excerpts of song lyrics, and references to illustrations. My presentation of juba here is not exhaustive as the term is historically so wide spread. It is possible that juba arrived in the Americas as a dance to which hand clapping was a part, and later became recognized solely as the type of hand clapping accompaniment for which it is best known.[15] African-styled rhythmic hand clapping is described first by travelers in Africa. Richard Jobson reported at length on the music and dance of Africans. He writes in one account about the circle surrounding the dancers he watched: "the standers by seeme to grace the dancer, by clapping their hands together after the manner of keeping time."[16] Former slave Henry Bibb, born in 1815 in Kentucky, mentions patting "juber" in his narrative, and dancing, singing, and playing the banjo, as deplorable activities encouraged by slaveholders.[17] Solomon Northup, in his *Twelve Years a Slave,* offers a description: "striking the hands on the knees, then striking the hands together, then striking the right shoulder with one hand, the left with the other—all the while keeping time with the feet, and singing."[18] Writer William B. Smith provided a description from a dance in Virginia before 1838. He saw "two athletic blacks . . . clapping Juber to the notes of the banjor. . . . The clappers rested the right foot on the heel, and its clap on the floor was in perfect unison with the notes of the banjor, and palms of the hands on the corresponding extremities."[19] A description by Lewis Paine from 1851 in Rhode Island shows how the practice of patting juba was truly a functional form of providing music for dance.

> This is done by placing one foot a little in advance of the other, raising the ball of the foot from the ground, and striking it in regular time, while, in connection, the hands . . . slightly together, and then upon the thighs, in this way they make the most curious noise, yet in such perfect order, it furnishes music to dance by. . . . It is really astonishing to witness the rapidity of their motions, their accurate time, and the precision of their music and dance. I have never seen it equaled in my life.[20]

In 1857, John Dixon Long found that the "plantation slaves. . . . Generally . . . have no instruments, but dance to the tunes and words of a leader, keeping time by striking their hands against the thighs, and patting the right foot."[21] Another analysis from the 1880s also points out that juba was a substitute for instruments. Sidney Lamier, in a discussion on the use of pauses in poetry, interprets how those patting juba as accompaniment

> for a comrade to dance by, venture upon quite complex successions of rhythm, not hesitating to syncopate, to change the rhythmic accent for a moment, or to indulge in other highly-specialized variations of the current rhythms. Here music . . . is in its rudest form, consisting of rhythm alone; for the patting is done with hands and feet, and of course no change of pitch or of tone-color is possible.[22]

Lamier concludes that juba is both rude and is rhythm alone, and to his ears there was no tone variation. Thomas Holly Chivers, writing to his friend Edgar Allan Poe around 1903, mentioned "a Jig which must be accompanied by a measured clapping of the thighs and alternately on each other. . . . There is no such rhythm as this in the Greek Poetry—none, in fact, in any other Nation under the sun. There is no dance in the world like that of Juba."[23]

Dr. John Wyeth, a slaveowner in Huntsville, Alabama, in the late nineteenth century, also described how juba was performed.

> there were accompanists who "patted" with the hands, keeping accurate time with the music. In patting, the position was usually a half-stoop or forward bend, with a slap of one hand on the left knee followed by the . . . right, and then a loud slap of the two palms together. I should add that the left hand made two strokes in half-time to one for the right, something after the double stroke of the left drumstick in beating the kettledrum.[24]

These detailed descriptions of juba show its role as a type of multiple percussion. That is, the accounts show clearly that a variety of sounds and therefore rhythms were possible from the use of the hands and feet and the various parts of the body. It is an interesting point that the drum set or traps, an American invention originated by African Americans in the early twentieth century, involves the use of all four limbs of the body in performance. It is as if the concepts of various sizes and types of percussion were already there in juba and were just waiting for the occasion to be put back onto real drums, in the form of traps, as there is no such grouping of drums in Africa. Contrary to Mr. Lamier's account, actually the purpose of this body percussion was to express as much tone and musical color variety as possible.

Lafcadio Hearn's account mentions juba in the context of dance. The following is a description from 1890 taken from the author's experiences in Cincinnati, Ohio.

> Sometimes the men advancing leaped and crossed legs with a double shuffle, and with almost sightless rapidity. Then the music changed to an old Virginia reel, and the dancing changing likewise, presented the most grotesque spectacle imaginable. The dancing became wild; men patted juba and shouted, the negro women danced with the most fantastic grace, their bodies describing almost incredible curves forward and backward; limbs intertwined rapidly in a wrestle with each other and with the music; the room presented a tide of swaying bodies and tossing arms, and flying hair.[25]

With Hearn, the "dance description" almost becomes a literary genre in itself. Along with contemporary chroniclers and professionals such as the luminary Charles Dickens, the verbal picturing of African Americans evolves.

Juba the percussive device, juba the dance, was also a song. William Smith, in his account, noted a song that the "clappers" sang, with lyrics that began "Juber up and Juber down, Juber all around de town."[26] Dr. John Wyeth, whose description of juba was just mentioned, also noted a song called Juba, with the following lyrics, that went with the dance.

*Juba dis and juba dat*
*Juba kill a yaller cat*
*Juba up and juba down*
*Juba runnin' all aroun'*[27]

Black musician and composer W. C. Handy's reminiscences provide other lyrics to juba.

*Juba jump and Juba sing,*
*Juba cut dat pigeon's wing;*
*Juba kick off Juba's shoe,*
*Juba dance dat Jubal Jew*[28]

Then what is juba? Or who is juba? In these song lyrics juba is possibly a person, or a type of person. Juba is "runnin' all aroun" and juba "kick[s] off Juba's shoe," but except for William Henry Lane, the free born black entertainer of the 1840s who became known as Master Juba, there are no other known prominent individuals of the time who took on this moniker. Juba as used in these lyrics could be the personification of the dance as well as a fictional character.

Juba could also be a reference to an African-based spirit of action, such as that described by playwright Paul Carter Harrison in the use of the word "nommo," or the more often quoted reference to the Yoruba term "ashe," the "power-to-make-things-happen."[29] Juba is generally not referred to as having a multiple existence as dance, song, person, thing in America, with a relationship to African Music and culture. Just as West African Hi-Life, Caribbean Calypso, and Brazilian Samba exist as music, dance, lifestyle, and are personified by leading entertainers, so possibly was juba in its day.

Juba was the subject of a number of illustrations of black culture in the nineteenth century. There are at least nine known representations of juba in scenes of African American culture from 1848 to 1876.[30] Of note are a depiction of Master Juba from the *Illustrated London News* in 1848, and "The Juba Dance" from "Old Maryland Homes and Ways," an article appearing in *The Century Magazine* in 1864.[31] Master Juba was known for his jig-like stepping and he is shown here in this way. "The Juba Dance" depicts one dancer in full view and another with only one foot visible, who are part of a scene with others waving, clapping, and watching the dancers. A fiddler is seated in the foreground. It is thought that juba the dance was a competitive dance of skill.[32] By comparison, where the Brazilian colonial era form of the capoeira masked martial arts in dance, Master Juba could be said to have masked violence itself in a physically aggressive dance form. This can also be said of hip hop break dancing. It is also known that Master Juba was known for his supremacy over any other dancer.[33] The two dancers in "The Juba Dance" could be competing.

It is also possible that these depictions are not associated with juba in any direct way. This writer does not know whether Master Juba admitted to dancing the juba, in whatever form. He was known as a popular vaudeville and minstrel show entertainer. Also "The Juba Dance" may have been titled in an arbitrary manner, for there is little that is definitive in its portrayals. These two depictions are still worthy of consideration because they are part of the continuum of knowing about and naming juba in American culture.

## The Shout

The shout is a religious ring or circular dance with song accompaniment. Its general characteristics are that participants walked, shuffled, and stamped in a rhythmic manner and for the most part did not lift their feet, bend their knees, cross their legs, or move their lower bodies in any way that could be considered secular. The rhythmic stamping was to accompany religious song. The performance of the religious ring shout was somewhat private or clandestine which accounts for the limited number of eyewitness descriptions.[34] The following will present descriptions and consider the purpose of the shout based on the accounts.

At a camp meeting in 1818 a group of white Quaker students witnessed black worshipers moving in a circle chanting "We're traveling to Immanuel's land, Glory! Halle-lu-jah." The students mentioned how a participant also blew a tin horn, and concluded that the slaves were acting out "Joshua's chosen men marching around the walls of Jericho, blowing the rams' horns and shouting, until the walls fell."[35] Sir Charles Lyell heard in 1845 about the difference between sacred and secular dancing among the slaves. Individuals reported to him that "Hit ain't railly dancin' 'less de feets is crossed," "dancin' ain't sinful iffen de foots ain't crossed."[36] Laura Towne, an educator who worked among former slaves on St. Helena Island beginning in 1862, presented a less sympathetic view. "Tonight I have been to a 'shout,' which seems to me certainly the remains of some old idol worship. . . . I never saw anything so savage. They call it a religious ceremony, but it seems more like a regular frolic to me."[37]

Thomas Wentworth Higginson, colonel and commander of the first black regiment in the Civil War, mentions the shout in his "Army Life in a Black Regiment," in a camp diary entry for December 11, 1862. "The everlasting 'shout' is always within hearing, with its mixture of piety and polka, and its castanet-like clapping of the hands."[38] In a section titled "Negro Spirituals," Higginson provides another description.

> Often in the starlit evening I have returned from some lonely ride by the swift river, or on the plover-haunted barrens, and, entering the camp, have silently approached some glimmering fire, round which the dusky figures moved in the rhythmical barbaric dance the negroes call a "shout," chanting, often harshly, but always in the most perfect time, some monotonous refrain.[39]

A writer who commented on African American culture often, H. G. Spaulding, witnessed in 1863 a shout that occurred after a praise meeting.

> Three or four, standing still, clapping their hands and beating time with their feet, commence singing in unison one of the peculiar shout melodies, while the others walk round in a ring, in single file, joining also in the song. Soon those in the ring leave off their singing, the others keeping it up the while with increased vigor, and strike into the shout step, observing most accurate time with the music. This step is something halfway between a shuffle and a dance, as difficult for an uninitiated person to describe as to imitate. At the end of each stanza of the song the dancers stop short with a slight stamp on the last note, and then, putting the other foot forward, proceed through the next verse. They will often dance to the same song for twenty or thirty minutes, once or twice, perhaps, varying the monotony of their movement by walking for a little while and joining in the singing. The physical exertion, which is really very great, as the dance calls into play nearly every muscle of the body, seems never to weary them in the least, and they frequently keep up a shout for hours, resting only for brief intervals between the different songs.[40]

William Francis Allen's collection *Slave Songs of the United States* presents an account of the shout taken from a newspaper article in *The Nation* for May 30, 1867. Allen's *Slave Songs* also included fully notated song texts.

> The true "shout" takes place on Sundays or on "praise" nights through the week, and either in the praise-house or in some cabin in which a regular religious meeting has been held . . . when the "sperichil" is struck up, [they] begin first walking and by-and-by shuffling round, one after the other, in a ring. The foot is hardly taken from the floor, and the progression is mainly due to a jerking, hitching motion, which agitates the entire shouter, and soon brings out streams of perspiration. . . . Song and dance are alike extremely energetic, and often, when the shout lasts into the middle of the night, the monotonous thud, thud of feet prevents sleep within half a mile of the praise house.[41]

Daniel Alexander Payne was a free black minister in the African Methodist Episcopal Church. He observed and tried to halt such religious meetings that he witnessed, and in his 1888 *Recollections of Seventy Years* he calls the groups "Rings" and "Fist and Heel Worshipers."

> About this time I attended a "bush meeting," where I went to please the pastor whose circuit I was visiting. After the sermon they formed a ring, and with coats off sung, clapped their hands and stamped their feet in a most ridiculous and heathenish way. I requested the pastor to go and stop their dancing. . . . After the sermon in the afternoon, having another opportunity of speaking alone to this young leader of the singing and clapping ring, he said: "Sinners won't get converted unless there is a ring." . . . Prayer was only a secondary thing, and this was rude and extravagant to the last degree. The man who had the most powerful pair of lungs was the one who made the best prayer, and he could be heard a square off. He who could sing the loudest and longest led the "Band," having his loins girded and a handkerchief in hand with which he kept time, while his feet resounded on the floor like the drum-sticks of a bass drum.[42]

Abigail Christensen, an observer writing in 1894, was moved to say that those "who have witnessed these shouts can never forget them."[43]

Interviews with former slaves reveal their participation in shouts and other ring dances, the secretive nature of some of the events, and the use of the drum at certain religious meetings. Hettie Campbell, a seventy-two-year-old resident of St. Mary's Island off the coast of South Carolina, talked to visitors, with her son Horace, in the late 1930s about "the old times."

> I do remembuh the big time we use tuh have wen I wuz young. We does plenty uh dances in those days. Dance roun in a ring. We has a big time long bout wen crops come in an everybody bring sumpin tuh eat wut

> they makes an we all gives praise fuh the good crop an then we shouts an sings all night. An wen the sun rise, we stahts tuh dance. It ain so long since they stop that back in the woods but these young people they does new kines uh dances.

Horace interjected here, "I seen em do those dances back in the woods but yuh." We asked what sort of music they had for the dances.

"They mosly have guitah now," said Hettie, "an we beats drums too. We makes em from coon hide stretched ovuh hoops. Muh step-fathuh, Andrew King, who lived down the Satilla Rivuh, use tuh tell me how it wuz in the ole days. He tell me they bring a boatload of them Africans ovuh."[44]

F. J. Jackson, "one of the oldest of the residents" of Grimballs Point, was asked about his memories of earlier times. "I use tuh go back tuh duh fahm on Satdy night fuh duh big times. Day hab wut yuh call shouts. . . . We use drum an fife an we made duh drum frum holluh beehive lawg."[45] Wallace Quarterman of Darien, also talked about his life.

> Ise bawn July 14, 1844, now figguh dat out fuh yuhsef, missus. Ise bawn at Sout Hampton, Libuty County, an I belong tuh Roswell King, but he done die long bout sometime in duh fifties and Ise sole fuh debt tuh Cunl Fred Waring on Skidaway Ilun. Ise bin bout fifteen wen I sen tuh Skidaway.
>
> We sho did hab big time goin tuh chuch in dose days. Not many uh deze Nigguhs kin shout tuhday duh way us could den. Yuh needs a drum fuh shoutin.
>
> We asked if they shouted to a drum then.
>
> We sho did. We beat a drum at duh chuch an we beat a drum on duh way tuh duh grabeyard tuh bury um. We walks in a long line moanin an we beats duh drum all duh way.[46]

Ryna Johnson of St. Simons Island spoke of her youth.

> Isa bout eight-five yeahs ole, but I cahn tell zackly. I belong tuh duh Coupers wen I wuk on duh plantation. It bin sech a long time I mos stop studiun bout dem days. But I membuh we use tuh hab good times. . . . Tings is sho change. Wen we is young, we use tuh hab big frolic an dance in a ring an shout tuh drum. Sometime we hab rattle made out uh dry good an we rattle em an make good music.[47]

The Slave Narrative informants help make clear that there was a shout in a real and practical sense, as in the words of Hettie Campbell and Horace, F. J. Jackson, Wallace Quaterman, and Ryna Johnson. Some of their versions of the shout were not necessarily related to religion and included the drum. Campbell speaks generally of a harvest ring dance. Jackson mentions the "shouts" in the context of Saturday night, Quaterman does mention the "shout" as a part of church, Ryna Johnson also speaks of a ring dance and "shout tuh drum" as connected to a "big frolic" and dance.

The broader case for the significance of the rhythmic qualities of the shout in the absence of musical instruments is made by the testimony here. The shout is placed in the sacred realm because of the clearly defined practice of not crossing the feet, as described by Sir Charles Lyell's informants. That the shout is percussive Thomas Wentworth Higginson mentions in his portrayal of the soldier's "rhythmic barbaric dance." H. G. Spaulding describes participants "beating time with their feet" and "observing most accurate time" with the "shout step."

Spaulding also comments on the shout continuing "for hours" as does William Francis Allen, who says the shout often "lasts into the middle of the night." Allen points out the "monotonous thud, thud of feet" that can be heard "within half a mile of the praise house." Daniel Alexander Payne, in spite of being appalled by the "Fist and Heel Worshipers," provides detailed descriptions observing that participants, after forming a ring, "clapped their hands and stamped their feet." Payne also points out how the prayer leader's feet "resounded on the floor like the drum-sticks of a bass drum."

## Horns

The use of horns by African Americans in early America was influenced by the same restrictions that existed for the drum. As Chapter Three shows, drum use continued within some black communities for the practical reasons of providing music for celebrations, funerals, and communication. Horns of various types are found in accounts in sanctioned uses, such as for calling slaves to work at plantations, but are also described in use among blacks for various other purposes. Some horns appear to be fixtures of rural or plantation life, the fog horn for example, and have little to do with African American culture. It is an intriguing aspect of life for blacks that these age-old ways of communication remained an integral part of their daily lives regardless of official restrictions or permissions. For the few accounts of the horn in use among African Americans, it remains a possibility that its function could have been like the drum's in other places and times.

To begin with an African account, John Howison presented impressions of the people he visited before 1834. "The amusements which the negroes most esteem next to conversation, are music and dancing. . . . Their musical instruments are drums, flutes, and horns, and a kind of rude guitar."[48] This description places the horn in the context of the other instruments often included in accounts of African music, that is, the drum and some type of stringed instrument.

Horns are most often described for communication and not to play tunes. In 1867 *Harper's Weekly* carried a piece titled "Scenes on a Cotton Plantation" that discussed a dance, prayer meeting, funeral, and the use of a horn as a call to work.[49] Irving E. Lowery, a minister and former slave, recounts in his *Life on the Old Plantation in Ante-Bellum Days* the horn calling workers to the fields at four o'clock in the morning.[50] An 1895 piece from *The New York Sun* titled "Corn Shuckin' Down South" includes a description of wooden bugles, five to six feet in length, that were used to call people together.[51]

One account discusses the blowing of a long tin horn to gather together a congregation, in the *Harper's Weekly* piece from 1880 titled "Inside Southern Cabins IV—Alabama, Agricultural Negroes."[52] The playing of conch shells is the subject of two pieces. One account from 1893 from the Georgia Sea Islands "The Legends of Jekyl Island" recalls the use of conch shells among the black population, and Basil Duke's *Reminiscences* describes the use of a "big conch shell" instead of the blowing of a horn to gather slaves.[53]

Two periodical illustrations depict horns played by blacks in two different settings. Edward King Smith's article "A Ramble in Virginia: From Bristol to the Sea," which appeared in *Scribner's Monthly Magazine* in 1884, included an illustration titled "The Summons to a Tobacco Sale" by artist J. Wells Champney. This piece shows a man playing a strait trumpet to announce the event.[54] Another piece appearing in *Frank Leslie's Illustrated Newspaper* in 1883 titled "The New South—Scenes in North Carolina, Georgia and Florida" is a full-page illustration of various scenes including "The Fog Horn—St. John's River."[55] A man is shown sitting high on what may be a dock, blowing a long straight horn in dark or near-dark conditions.

This group of accounts shows the place of the horn in agrarian settings as a tool of communication. The description referring to the calling of a religious congregation is unique, and the other accounts are certainly within context for a rural plantation setting. These examples show the variety of instruments of communication, other than the drum, in use among slaves.

## Bells

Following are descriptions of two images that show signal bells in use on plantations for communication. One illustration, titled "The Plantation Bell" by artist E. W. Kemble, appeared in the article "Sugar-Making in Louisiana," which appeared in *The Century Magazine* in 1887.[56] The illustration shows an elderly black man pulling a rope to ring a large bell that is hung in an open wooden frame tower that has a small roof over the bell.

The accompanying article does not mention the bell, and is a survey of the Southern sugar industry, the life of sugar planters, and the lifestyle on such plantations. This twenty-page piece has eighteen illustrations.

The second piece is an illustration that appears in a contemporary documentary collection titled *The Social Implications of Early Negro Music* by Bernard Katz.[57] The illustration is not identified as accompanying any work in the collection but is included between chapters. The illustration shows a woman pulling a chain that is attached to a bell hung on a post and frame, on which also hangs a sign that reads "Taylor House, J.A. Jarvis, Proprietor." In the background is what appears to be a wood frame house with a porch and stairs leading to the front door. Although this picture is not identified, it is, because of its context, a nineteenth-century depiction.

These illustrations add to our understanding of the aural environment of the plantation slave. Although certain types of communication were banned, other agriculture-related or European American based systems were in use, such as a tobacco sale horn or a plantation signal bell. That horns or conch shells were used among blacks then is not surprising. The use of horns and bells in these written and visual examples speaks also to the work and leisure rhythms of black life during slavery. Slave time was thus defined by the types of sounds, calls, and signals on any given day of the week. It then becomes almost essential that blacks would have their own system of clandestine communication. How could they not?[58]

## Stringed Instruments

### *The Violin*

Of the stringed instruments in use among African Americans, the violin and banjo maintained an important role and were not played necessarily to substitute for the drum. Although, it can be said, that the rhythmic capabilities of these instruments were in fact a surrogate. The violin, the most used of all slave instruments, was in fact accompanied by the stick-playing straw beaters mentioned earlier in this chapter. The popularity of the violin is contrary to the belief that the banjo was the central instrument of early American blacks.[59] Straws "used to beat on the fiddles" and "broom-straws on fiddle-strings" therefore made the violin a party to a kind of substitute drumming in spite of this instrument's melodic role in music generally. The fiddles in use were not all of the European type, as the following descriptions demonstrate.

Another depiction from Bernard Katz's *Social Implications*, appearing between chapters, shows a young black male sitting near an opening in a rough straw or lean-to type abode, playing a homemade violin.[60] The instrument has a bow made from a branch that has been bent and strung, and the body of the instrument is straight and box-like and does not resemble the European-styled violin. Numerous fiddles exist in African music that are played with bows and held in a variety of positions different from the European violin.[61] This player is holding his "fiddle" in a proper violin position. This unknown work from the nineteenth century shows a homemade or non-Western version of the fiddle. As physical evidence of a particularly African American approach to the violin, there is a "gourd-bodied fiddle" that was an item in the Cleveland Museum of Art's 1978 exhibition "The Afro-American Tradition in Decorative Arts." This fiddle dates from the early twentieth century in the Upper Shenandoah Valley of Virginia, and is a long tubular gourd to which a European-styled violin neck, bridge, and tailpiece has been added.[62] This instrument suggests, in its mixing of materials, another type of substitution or surrogate use.

To compare with these African-styled fiddles, artist E. W. Kemble produced a depiction of a black violinist titled "The Fiddler" that appeared in 1887 in James Lane Allen's "Mrs. Stowe's 'Uncle Tom' at Home in Kentucky." This article, which appeared in *The Century Magazine*, addresses the change in the culture of African Americans since the Civil War as compared to Harriet Beecher Stowe's fictionalized antebellum characters. The drawing shows a fiddler sitting in a chair on a platform under a large tree. He is dressed in a jacket and string tie and is at rest with his violin under his arm. Four well-dressed whites stand in conversation in the background, and the corner of a large house is visible. The fiddler is pictured as erudite, and it is worthy of note that he is the sole musician, and therefore may have provided the "time" for the dancers. In contrast to the homespun fiddler, this gentleman appears almost as a European classical musician, which of course may have been the intention of this depiction, for the humor of the Northern readers of *The Century*. Despite the subtleties of interpretation, such illustrations imply the functional and rhythmic role of the fiddler.[63]

In the Caribbean, where the use of the drum was allowed to some extent among slaves, there are also examples of the use of the violin in more acculturated settings. The following two accounts show a separation in the types of instruments. The African drum was used in one setting, and the European violin for a different type of music and dance. The first account is from 1790.

> Their music is composed of any thing that makes a tinkling sound; a hollow cane, or bamboo, with holes in it, in imitation of a fife, an herring-barrel, or tub, with sheep-skins substituted for the heads, in imitation of a drum, called a gumbay; but sometimes more 'grandy balls,' as they are called, are honoured with a taboret and violin.[64]

This description is from Jamaica in 1823.

> Their music is very rude; it consists of the goombay or drum, several rattles, and the voices of the female slaves, which, by the way, is the best part of the music. . . . The drums of the Africans vary in shape . . . according to the different countries, as does also their vocal music. In a few years it is probable that the rude music here described will be altogether exploded among the creole negroes, who shew a decided preference for European music. Its instruments, its tunes, its dances, are now pretty generally adopted by the young creoles. . . . A sort of subscription balls are set on foot, and parties of both sexes assemble and dance country dances to the music of a violin, tambarine . . . this improvement of taste is in a great measure confined to those who are, or have been domestics about the houses of the whites, and have in consequence imbibed a fondness for their amusements, and some skill in the performance.[65]

African Americans, then, adapted the violin to both Old World and New World uses.

### *The Banjo*

The banjo is an African American invention that was a hybrid of various African stringed instruments.[66] Benjamin Latrobe drew a picture of an African-styled stringed instrument resembling a banjo in one of his sketches from Congo Square, New Orleans, in 1819.[67] In New York's Metropolitan Museum is an example of an early handmade banjo. This banjo used drum technology, that is, there is an animal skin tacked to the top of a hollowed-out gourd, although the neck of the instrument is flat and has a sculpted surface on it that resembles a European instrument.[68] Both the Cleveland Museum's fiddle and the Metropolitan Museum's banjo are simply African instruments with a European neck attached. The resonator, the sound producer, the heart of the instrument, is African. The fingerboard, or manipulator, is an adaptation.

Because of the banjo's African origins, it is natural that it would have a percussive role.[69] There is little surprise then in the fact that blacks would become more associated in the minds of Americans with this instrument than with any other. There are in the record accounts of the violin and banjo in performance with and without the drum, and in every conceivable combination of instruments available to blacks. Most interesting, as a precursor to the twentieth-century phenomenon of jazz, are the music ensembles that utilized violin and/or banjo with hand percussion instruments such as tambourine and bones. The combination of percussion instruments suggests a kind of "rhythm section" long before jazz.

Before the drum reemerged in the early twentieth century, African Americans could only practically utilize what was inexpensive, small, and portable. This conclusion is reinforced by the fact that in the development of the minstrel show in the nineteenth century, what is known as the "half-circle," an arrangement of players who sat facing the audience to perform, consisted of just such a grouping of instruments. Stringed instruments and hand percussion became identified with black music performance because of the limitations put in place by the prohibitions of slavery.[70]

Two illustrations provide examples of the types of stringed instruments and percussion that were in use in the nineteenth century, both among blacks and on the minstrel stage, and what meaning the choice of instruments may have had. A lithograph from about 1850 of "The Ethiopian Serenaders," a blackface minstrel group, shows an ensemble of five men seated on a stage playing bones, two banjos, accordion, and tambourine.[71] "Bones" were two sticks, originally animal rib bones, later rosewood, that were played in one hand as a set. The tambourine has been described as a "small hand drum" although it is not normally considered a drum.[72] These white males who were imitating blacks thus chose what was believed to be the typical instrumentation within the stilted image of black performers that was the basis of minstrelsy.

A drawing from *Frank Leslie's Illustrated Newspaper* of 1872 titled "Wandering Minstrels on Harlem Lane" shows a group of four African Americans performing on bones, violin, banjo, and tambourine. One of the men appears to be singing.[73] In the accompanying story, the writer describes the performance of a group of four "negro minstrels" in "the barroom of Smith's Club House." The musicians are "always well received," and "certainly exhibit industry in picking up the latest songs, stories and fancy steps." The patrons include "liberal-hearted men and women who frequent Harlem Lane on pleasant moonlight nights, in jaunty cutters and behind enviable steeds." The caption at the bottom of the drawing is "Life Sketches in the Metropolis—Wandering African Minstrels Performing at a Noted Place of Resort on Harlem Lane—From a Sketch by John N. Hyde" and the piece has the signature "Hyde" on the lower left. Publications such as Leslie's were known for their staff artists who did "life sketches," particularly during the Civil War, and, from on location in the South, to record conditions for Northern readers. This type of ensemble is the most described, generally, from colonial times to the twentieth century, and the emphasis on rhythm instruments is usually present. This configurations of instruments make all the more sense because drums and horns were for the most part out of circulation among blacks.[74]

Not only is the banjo a part of ensembles that were made up of other rhythm instruments, but a number of accounts describe the drum-like quality of the banjo itself in performance. James Fenimore Cooper portrays a Pinkster Day celebration in New York in 1757 in his fictionalized *Satanstoe*. Pinkster Day was a uniquely Northern African American celebration that was named after Pentecost Sunday and occurred at that time of year.[75] Up "near the head of Broadway, on the common," he explains:

> nine-tenths of the blacks in the city, and the whole country within thirty or forty miles, indeed, were collected in thousands in those fields, beating banjos, singing African songs, drinking, and worst of all, laughing in a way that seemed to set their very hearts rattling within their ribs.[76]

Cooper goes on to write about African drumming at these events as what "distinguish a Pinkster frolic." But it is interesting that the author characterizes the banjos as being beat upon. Not only is the piece racist, it is a form of social satire on an insinuated black majority and their possession of aural space through performance, and even via their laughter. It is possible that the performers presented the cultural remnants of their past, although only what a racist Northern society would allow. The conclusion can be made also that these whites were seeing the beginnings of a new African society in the Americas, a rich hybrid of the originals.

An account of the music and dance of Congo Square, New Orleans in 1846 that appeared in the New Orleans *Daily Picayune* similarly characterizes the banjo.

> In various parts of the square a number of male and female negroes assemble, dressed in their holiday clothes, with the very gayest bandanna handkerchiefs upon the heads of the females, and, accompanied by the thumping of a banjo or drum . . . perform the most grotesque African dances.[77]

Here the thumping of the banjo and drum are synonymous. In a description of the Calenda dance from around 1882, J. W. Buel recalled the motions of a female dancer and the sounds of the music and singing[78]

> with a body waving and undulating like [a] . . . snake. . . . Confining herself to a spot not more than two feet in space, she began to sway on one and the other side. Gradually the undulating motion was imparted to her body from the ankles to the hips. Then she tore the white handkerchief from her forehead. This was a signal, for the whole assembly

> sprang forward and entered the dance. The beat of the drum, the thrum of the banjo, swelled louder and louder. . . . Above all the noise rose. . . .
>
> Hounm! dance Calinda,
> Voudou! Magnian,
> Aie! Aie!
> Dance Calinda!

The context of the banjo here shows its use with the drum in what could only be a rhythmic "thrum" that gained in volume at the height of this so-called ceremony.

A *Leslie's Illustrated* story that appeared in 1883 is titled "A Night Scene in Lynchburg, Va." and describes the opening of the tobacco markets for the season. While "negro and other small cultivators" await the opening, they "indulge their fun-loving tendencies by characteristic merry-makings." Five men and one boy are around a campfire, some are sitting while others stand. One man dances before the blaze as two musicians, one playing banjo, the other playing bones, accompany him. Two men are playing a game of cards as others watch. This work, which was a cover illustration, shows again a stereotyped scene of African American instrumentation and dance where banjo and bones supply melody and rhythm.[79]

## Notes

1 See, The Music of Africa chapter six, pp. 69–84.
2 In *Black Dance*, Lynne Emery attempts to account for the transition to an African American culture without drums. p. 80.
3 The selections for this discussion are taken from the section in Traditions on the WPA Slave Narrative Collection, pp. 208–17. The original source is George P. Rawick, *The American Slave: A Composite Autobiography* (Westport, 1972).
4 This is in an account from Mississippi in volume seven of the Slave Narratives. See, Eileen Southern, *African-American Traditions in Song, Sermon, Tale, and Dance, 1600s–1920* (Westport, 1990), 214.
5 See, Federal Writers' Project, Slave Narratives. IV, Part 1, p. 227, In Lynne Emery, *Black Dance in the United States from 1619 to 1970* (Princeton, 1972), 84.
6 Dena Epstein also takes note of the use of rhythm instruments other than the drum in North America. "The omnipresent drums of the West Indies were not heard on the mainland—not even at slave dances, where other percussive devices (sticks, bones, tambourines, and clapping) had to take their place." See, Dena J. Epstein, *Sinful Tunes and Spirituals: Black Folk Music to the Civil War* (Chicago, 1977), 144.
7 Mary Scott Saint-Armand, *A Balcony in Charleston*, (Richmond, 1941). See, *Sinful Tunes* 159.
8 William Cullen Bryant, *Letters* (New York, 1850). See, *Traditions* 326 and *Sinful Tunes* 144.

9 Elizabeth Cexe, *Memories* (1912). See, *Sinful Tunes* 144.
10 Ronald Killion, *Slavery Time* (Savannah, 1973). Interview by Savah Hall in 1937. See, *Sinful Tunes* 145.
11 Matthew Lewis. *Journal of a West India Proprietor, 1815–1817* (New York, 1929). See, *Black Dance* 18. and *Sinful Tunes* 52.
12 Alcee Fortier, "Customs and Superstitions in Louisiana," *Journal of American Folklore* (July 1888). See, *Sinful Tunes* 135.
13 George Washington Cable, "The Dance in Place Congo," *Century Magazine* 31 (February 1886). See, *Black Dance* 158.
14 Elizabeth W. Allston Pringle, *A Woman Rice Planter* (New York: Macmillan, 1913). See, Traditions 230.
15 There are varying views on the origins of juba. See, *Sinful Tunes* 141. See "The Negro Dance," in *The Negro Caravan Sterling Brown* (New York, 1941). See, *Black Dance* 96. Harold Courlander, *Haiti Singing* (Chapel Hill, 1939). See, *Black Dance* 57.
16 Richard Jobson, *The Golden Trade* (London, 1623). See, *Sinful Tunes* 141.
17 Henry Bibb, *Narrative* (New York, 1849). See, *Sinful Tunes* 142.
18 Solomon Northup, *Twelve Years a Slave* (New York, 1853). See, *Sinful Tunes* 142.
19 William B. Smith, "The Persimmon Tree and the Beer Dance," *Farmer's Register* 6 (1 April, 1838), 58–61. See, *Sinful Tunes* 143.
20 Lewis W. Paine, *Six Years in a Georgia Prison: Narrative of Lewis W. Paine, Who Suffered Imprisonment Six Years in Georgia, for the Crime of Aiding the Escape of a Fellowman from that State, after He Had Fled from Slavery*. Written By Himself (New York, 1851). See, Traditions 17.
21 John Dixon Long, *Pictures of Slavery*, (Philadelphia, 1857). See, *Sinful Tunes* 143.
22 Sidney Lamier, *The Science of English Verse* (New York, 1880). See, *Sinful Tunes* 142.
23 George Weedberry, "The Poe-Chivers Papers," *Century Magazine* 65 (January 1903). See, *Sinful Tunes* 142.
24 John Allen Wyeth, *With Sabre and Scalpel* (New York, 1914). See, *Sinful Tunes* 96.
25 Lafcadio Hearn, *Two Years in the French West Indies* (New York: Harper, 1890). See, *Black Dance* 146.
26 See, "Persimmon Tree," in *Sinful Tunes* 143.
27 See, Sabre in *Sinful Tunes* 96.
28 W. C. Handy, *Blues: An Anthology* (New York, 1926). See, *Black Dance* 97.
29 Paul Carter Harrison's, *The Drama of Nommo* (New York: Grove Press, 1972). is in large part an assessment or the vital force behind African and African American creativity. Robert Farris Thompson describes the term "ashe" as used by *The Yoruba in Flash of the Spirit* (New York: Vintage, 1984), 5–9.
30 Southern's Traditions provides a survey of visual depictions of African American culture.
31 "'Master Juba' at Vauxhall Gardens, London," *Illustrated London News* (5 August, 1848) See, *Black Dance* 187. See, "The Juba Dance" by artist Howard Helmick in "Old Maryland Homes and Ways" by John Williamson Palmer. *The Century Magazine* 49/2 (December 1864), 256.
32 Katherine Dunham discusses the African and Caribbean origins of juba in "The Negro Dance," in *The Negro Caravan*, ed. Sterling Brown (New York, 1941). See, *Black Dance* 96.

33 See, *Black Dance* 85–90.

34 Regarding the small number of existing accounts of the shout See, *Sinful Tunes* 233.

35 Don Yoder, *Pennsylvania Spirituals* (Lancaster, 1961). See, Lawrence Levine, *Black Culture and Black Consciousness: Afro-American Folk Thought from Slavery to Freedom* (Oxford and New York, 1977), 37–38.

36 Sir Charles Lyell, *A Second Visit to the United States of North America* (New York, 1894). See, Black Culture 38.

37 *Letters and Diary of Laura M. Towne: Written from the Sea Islands of South Carolina, 1862–1884*, ed. Rupert Sargent Holland (Cambridge, MA, 1912). See, Black Culture 141.

38 Thomas Wentworth Higginson, *Army Life in a Black Regiment* (Boston, 1870). See, Eileen Southern, ed., *Readings in Black American Music* (New York: W.W. Norton, 1971), 164.

39 See, *Army Life* in Eileen Southern's *Readings* 173.

40 H. G. Spaulding, "Under the Palmetto," *Continental Monthly* 4 (July–December 1863). 197. See, *Black Dance* 123.

41 William Allen, Charles Ware, and Lucy Garrison, *Slave Songs of the United States* (New York, 1867). See, Eileen Southern, *The Music of Black Americans: A History* (New York: W. W. Norton, 1997), 182. In her discussion of the shout Southern finds that the "only missing element was the instrumental music of drums and string instruments, and to a certain extent this was compensated for by the hand clapping of the singers." p. 183.

42 Daniel Alexander Payne, *Recollections of Seventy Years* (Nashville, 1888). See, Readings 65–70.

43 Abigail Holmes Christensen, "Spirituals and 'Shouts' of Southern Negroes," *Journal of American Folklore* 7 (1894). See, *Black Culture* 38.

44 See, Writers' Program, *Georgia: Drums and Shadows; Survival Studies among the Georgia Coastal Negroes [by the] Savannah Unit, Georgia Writers' Project, Work Projects Administration* (Athens, 1940), 178.

45 See, Ibid. 92.

46 See, Ibid. 141.

47 See, Ibid. 168.

48 John Howison, *European Colonies in Various Parts of the World, Viewed in Their Social, Moral, and Physical Condition*, (London: R. Bentley, 1834). See, *Sinful Tunes* 7.

49 "Scenes of a Cotton Plantation," *Harper's Weekly* 11 (2 February, 1867), 69. See, Traditions cite 994.

50 Irving E. Lowery, *Life on the Plantation in Ante-Bellum Days* (Columbia, SC, 1991). See, Traditions cite 1961.

51 "Corn Shuckin' Down South," *The New York Sun* (11 November, 1895), 4. See, Traditions cite 595.

52 Eliza Frances Andrews, "Inside Southern Cabins, IV: Alabama, Agricultural Negroes," *Harper's Weekly* 24 (4 December, 1880), 781–2. See, Traditions cite 726.

53 Franklin H. Head, "The Legends of Jekyl Island," *New England Magazine* 8 (May 1893), 393–9. See, *Traditions and Duke, Basil Reminiscences of General Basil W. Duke, C.S.A. Doubleday* (New York, 1911). See, Traditions cite 1873.

54 Edward King Smith, "A Ramble in Virginia: From Bristol to the Sea," *Scribner's Monthly Magazine* 7 (April 1884). See, Traditions cite 1497.

55 C. Upham, "The New South: Scenes in North Carolina, Georgia and Florida," *Frank Leslie's Illustrated Newspaper* 56 (March 1883). See, *Traditions* 1611.
56 "Sugar-Making in Louisiana," *The Century Magazine* 35/1 (November, 1887), 100–20.
57 Bernard Katz's, *The Social Implications of Early Negro Music in the United States* (New York: Arno Press, 1969), 22.
58 I have long had an interest in time and the cycles of time in the preindustrial world. My reference for the discussion here has been English historian E. P. Thompson's "Time Work-Discipline, and Industrial Capitalism." *Past and Present* no. 38.
59 Eileen Southern has shown in *Readings in Black American Music*, using a sample of slave advertisements for runaways, that the violin was the most mentioned instrument that slaves were skilled upon. See, pp. 31–5.
60 See, *Social Implications* 24.
61 See, *The Music of Africa*, chapter nine, for a discussion of bowed stringed instruments.
62 See, *The Afro-American Tradition in Decorative Arts. Notes on the Exhibition.* Cleveland Museum of Art. 1978.
63 See, James Lane Allen, "Mrs. Stowe's 'Uncle Tom' at Home in Kentucky," *The Century* 34/6 (October 1887), 852–67.
64 J. B. Moreton, *Manners and Customs in the West India Islands*, (London, 1790). See, *Sinful Tunes* 83.
65 John Stewart, *A View of the Past and Present State of the Island of Jamaica; with Remarks on the Moral and Physical Condition of the Slaves, and on the Abolition of Slavery in the Colonies* (Edinburgh: Oliver & Boyd, 1823). See, *Sinful Tunes* 85.
66 Dena Epstein provides one interpretation in "The Folk Banjo: A Documentary History," *Ethnomusicology* 19 (September 1975), 347–71.
67 Sketches from the manuscript journal of Benjamin Latrobe. Entry for February 21, 1819, from New Orleans, describing "the assembly of Negro . . . every Sunday . . . on the Common." The Papers of Benjamin Henry Latrobe. Maryland Historical Society. *Sinful Tunes* 98.
68 Banjo circa 1840 from William Boucher, Jr., Baltimore. The Metropolitan Museum of Art. New York. The Crosby Brown Collection of Musical Instruments. See, *The Art of Music, American Painting and Musical Instruments, 1770–1910* (Hamilton College, 1984).
69 Of the five hundred and sixty-three citations that have made up the basis for this study, thirty mention the playing of the banjo in some type of group instrumental setting. Thirteen of the accounts describe the banjo in performance with the drum; twenty discuss the banjo in a group without the drum but with some other type of percussion.
70 This conclusion is similar to a point that Lynne Emery makes. "Accompanied, then, by a banja (or benza, bonjour, or homemade banjo), a calabash or gourd filled with pebbles, and a baboula (or goombay, gomba, cotter, or board played with sticks or hands)—and sometimes a jawbone rubbed by a stick or bone—the Negro slaves sang, clapped, and danced." See, *Black Dance* 20.
71 "The Ethiopian Serenaders." Lithograph circa 1850. See, *Art of Music* 26.
72 Frederick R. Selch, author of "The Musical Instruments: A Brief History," which appears in *The Art of Music*, provides these descriptions of bones and tambourine. See, *Art of Music* 27.
73 "Wandering Minstrels on Harlem Lane," *Leslie's Illustrated* 34/862 (6 April, 1872), story p. 60, illus. p. 61.

74 Lynne Emery and Dena Epstein corroborate this conclusion regarding the makeup of slave instrumental groups. See, *Black Dance* 86. See, *Sinful Tunes* 119.
75 Lynne Emery discusses the origin of Pinkster Day in *Black Dance* 141.
76 James Fenimore Cooper, *Satanstoe* (New York, 1856). See, *Black Dance* 141.
77 See, *Black Dance* 160.
78 James William Buel, *Metropolitan Life Unveiled; or the Mysteries and Miseries of America's Great Cities, Embracing New York, Washington City, San Francisco, Salt Lake City, and New Orleans* (St. Louis, 1882). See, *Black Dance* 168.
79 "A Night Scene in Lynchburg, Va," *Leslie's Illustrated* (1883).

# Epilogue

## Primitivism's Disconnect

A hierarchical view of culture has over time had an effect on how the West has valued people's practices. As a force, modernism's primitive bent, beginning at the beginning of the twentieth century, began to value the art of tribal cultures as containing elements equally expressive yet unusual to Europe. Primitivism sought an alternative aesthetic, although as an artistic evolutionary path turned few of its discoveries into lasting concepts. Cubism borrowed from the industrial, and there was little beyond the adoption of the trope of the tribal (see Illustration 5.1).[1] The lament here is that non-Western cultures have been continually misconstrued. Houston Baker writes that one possible strategy for defining modernism is as the "primitive structural underpinnings of a putatively civilized mankind."[2] Baker's comment, I believe, rightly presents a modernist commitment to the primitive that becomes evident in the early twentieth century. Primitivism is the West's fantasy. What I will call the "disconnect" of primitivism is that contiguous, changing, improvisatory ideas are presented as representative, fixed notions. William Francis Allen wrote down hymns that he heard African Americans sing and published them in "Slave Songs of the United States" (1867). An oral song form instantly became set on paper. The spiritual was born, and, possibly, it ended. There are many variations to the songs that African Americans were singing at the time. Allen's set may have had the reality of instigating the disappearance of an ultimately variable form. Over time, spirituals became widespread and standardized.[3] In the visual arts, Pablo Picasso's "Bust of a Woman" (1909) mimics the sculptural aspects of African and Oceanic art. Our conception of the primitive mask is limited, in truth, to the arbitrary collecting and whims of art dealers in Paris at the turn of the last century. The application of the form has shown little variation.[4] In jazz, with the recording of musicians and their creative flights, beginning in the early twentieth century, the copied, repeated note-for-note, and

*Illustration 5.1* "Invitation to a Dada Evening." 1916.

Source: Marcel Janco. 1916. *Women in Dada: Essays on Sex, Gender, and Identity*. Naomi Sawelson-Gorse. 1998. p. 303.

"sampled" solo became common. This is actually contrary to the spirit of the form. There are more Charlie Parkers in this world, referring to the famous alto saxophone innovator, than Mr. Parker could have ever imagined. In jazz it is an affront to take someone else's ideas, although in the name of commerce, the practice has, in effect, prevailed. The reference that I am making here is dependent on technology, in the ability to duplicate, and, in markets, with buyers' willingness to view, possess, or listen to the duplications. The separation, the disconnect, is that these folk forms, not part of a largely white consumer society, become so. The concept of primitivism is by nature a presentation of accessibility and consumption. Primitivism sought the unattainable.

In *Western Music and its Others: Difference, Representation, and Appropriation in Music* (2000), editor Georgina Born writes regarding the "presence of difference and repetition in vernacular culture." Houston Baker's "deformation of mastery" and Henry Louis Gates Jr.'s "signifyin(g)" are ideas that form the basis of points made regarding a view of a kind of reversal in the music. For the Duke Ellington orchestra and the music of South African jazz pianist Abdullah Ibrahim, the complexity of their art rejects a simplistic view, writes contributor Richard Middleton.[5] The idea of "ethnographic modernism," a phrase used by contemporary anthropologist James Clifford, is put forth by Kurt Eisen in *Theatrical Ethnography and Modernist Primitivism in Eugene O'Neill and Zora Neale Hurston* (2008). The goal of early twentieth-century anthropologists such as Franz Boas, writes Eisen, was to connect "the material lives of primitive peoples and civilized readers to enact a kind of deep cultural unconscious, enabling readers to understand themselves as both produced by and distinctly individuated from their own cultural circumstances." In this vein the author critiques the approaches of playwright Eugene O'Neill and writer and dramatist Zora Neale Hurston. To quote Clifford, "a state of being in culture while looking at culture" became the modernist mode. Eisen continues that plays such as *The Emperor Jones* (1920) presented white audiences with alienation. Alternatively, Hurston deploys "mimicry" to recreate familiar, and understood, settings. Where O'Neill was in a search for the primitive, Hurston had already arrived, and sought to share, to translate. Hurston's comic and often quoted passage in the essay "How it Feels to be Colored Me" (1928) features a description of a personal metaphorical jaunt in the jungle, while listening to jazz, at the expense of her white companion. In this sense, the clichéd view of the consumption of hip hop has continued the form, offering young, white, suburban males a slice of a culture that they are categorically not invited to participate in. Another modern aspect might be that, like jazz, primitive drama was a consumable: the primitive became an option, a resource, a purchasable way of being or experience.[6] In an example for Europe, with reference specific to Germany, Berndt Ostendorf in "Subversive Reeducation? Jazz as a Liberating Force in Germany and Europe" writes regarding the "shock of the new" that was jazz.

The new music spoke to the agendas of futurism, surrealism, Dada, primitivism, radical democracy, multiculturalism, and cosmopolitanism and ushered in a new way of being—all at once. But it gave to these high cultural transgressions a decidedly vernacular spin thus preparing a structure of feeling for the subsequent victory of a popular culture industry.

Ostendorf suggests that black music served to radicalize Europe and to instigate cultural innovation even in the face of a considerable critique.[7]

Amazingly, this relation to the actions of African Americans fused not only pleasant performance into the psyche. The black body remained, literally, a site on which terror was perpetrated. In "Racial Violence, 'Primitive'

Music, and the Blues Entrepreneur: W. C. Handy's Mississippi Problem" (2002), Adam Gussow presents the wrenching story of the practice of lynching and how the African American instrumentalist, composer, and entrepreneur William Christopher Handy was exposed to the death of fellow blacks in his travels. "Modern technologies of vision" such as photography is one example of a "field of vision" within which the staged act of lynching occurred. The act "simultaneously communalizes white power and territorializes the black body." The author points to how Handy and fellow musicians reversed the daily oppression of the Jim Crow South by mocking whites while amongst themselves. Handy's class position separated him from the itinerant blues performer that was his model.[8] His link to the primitive was not controlled or predictable to the extent that the environments of Zora Neal Hurston may have been. Indeed, his proximity to terror is more real than previously alluded to by Paul Gilroy's phrase. For Clara Henderson in "'When Hearts Beat Like Native Drums:' Music and the Sexual Dimensions of the Notions of 'Savage' and 'Civilized' in Tarzan and His Mate, 1934" (2001), the notion of terror and the primitive is fictionalized for the film medium. In the film, African men and women are shown nude "as part of the ambient backdrop of [a] homogeneous savage environment." The bare skin of the white male and female performers are censored. His hips and her breasts, Weissmuller and O'Sullivan, are cut from final versions. Drumming is used in the soundtrack of the film and here are scenes in which African porters "draw back in terror, some falling to the ground in fright." The drums bring warriors out of hiding for a battle scene in the film. Henderson mentions how the film soundtrack is overpowered and becomes "a muddled confusion of noise." The author also presents an analysis of the tritone, the flatted-fifth in jazz, and how the interval was linked to the devil historically in Western Europe and how "a mood of disorientation and chaos" result from the stylized use of the tritone in the film.[9]

In *African-American Performance and Theater History* (2001), Harry Justin Elam, in an introduction, presents race in theatrical terms. Race is a "device" that is only one of a set that is "co-constructed." Belief is both created and suspended in performance. In a chapter titled "Deep Skin: Reconstructing Congo Square," Joseph Roach describes how white observers of historic performance were distracted by skin color from "cultural productions" that they observed. The author's take on the nature of observation suggests that performance itself becomes essentialized by race. Art cannot be separated from social values. In his essay, history and memory are rooted in performance.[10] In "The Jewish Entertainer as Cultural Lightning Rod: The Case of Lenny Bruce" (1997), Maria Damon explores the marginalizing, reducing, alienating aspects of the shaped image of the ethnic entertainer in America. The author finds that Bruce was sexualized in a negative and predatory way. His language was eventually labeled obscene, and he and it were censored. Not so much primitive as exotic, the loose cannon aspect of Bruce's language and his "seduction" and "attack" approach to the audience made for controversy. His 1962 obscenity trial focused in part on the spoken word piece "To is a preposition, come is a verb." What Damon calls Bruce's "tragicomic spiel" was in a classic comic sense self-deprecating, but, as delivered by this man, at this time the content was viewed as subversive. In the very sense that this section began, Lenny Bruce's creative flow was captured, fixed, and judged.[11]

## The Imagination

African Americans sought to connect to their past in the early twentieth century. Particularly, writers identified with the Harlem Renaissance articulated relationships, literal and symbolic, with their African past. In *Imagining Home: Class, Culture, and Nationalism in the African Diaspora* (1994), contributor Kathy Ogren's "'What is Africa to Me?': African Strategies in the Harlem Renaissance" presents material to suggest that some writers sought practical connections to the past. For example, Alain Locke's collection *The New Negro* (1925) features the view of various scholars. In it, Arthur Schomburg made a case for the need for African Americans to create an accurate history of their African past, and anthropologist Arthur Huff Fauset called for a professional approach to collecting and understanding folklore. Locke's essay suggested the inspirational use of the African arts for African Americans. His article featured photos of African masks. Ogren mentions "dissociative" writers such as Mellville Heskovits, whose essay focused on the African American present in America. She notes that in this early twentieth-century collection there was no comparative analysis of Africa alongside discussions of social, political, and educational issues at home.[12]

In Kofi Agawu's 1995 article "The Invention of African Rhythm," appearing in the *Journal of the American Musicological Society*, the author describes the relation between African peoples and the idea of rhythmic practices. Agawu traces from the colonial era in Africa how Europeans had always been dumbfounded at the complexity of African rhythm and yet minimalized it as merely exotic. By the mid-twentieth century, scholars finally became sympathetic to the value of African music as cultural expression, yet, ending with the scholar Richard Alan Waterman, there is still the language of incomprehension. Agawu goes further to say that important African scholars of the music, including J. H. Nketia in *The Music of Africa* (1974), also cast rhythm as an overall aspect of African culture. This focus on rhythm has pushed aside other aspects of African performance such as the relation of song and dance, the visual, textile, and costume aspects and function, and the role of the music in society. Agawu finds that "'African rhythm,' then, is an invention, a construction, a fiction, a myth, ultimately a lie."[13]

Agawu's critique is not new in the sense of an expression of how the black arts have always been compared to the culture of America and Western Europe. Can black expression be described without the white world? Can we imagine a multicultural world not dominated by the West? In *The Black Atlantic* (1993), Paul Gilroy considers authenticity in jazz and brings up the notion of interpretation among musicians, the Miles Davis and Wynton Marsalis debate regarding innovation versus custodianship. Then Gilroy describes the conundrum of origins in popular music. An example of this idea is the American group No Doubt, which began with Gwen Stefani as vocalist, and their apparent roots in Jamaican Ska music, when most people in the U.S. had never heard of the form.

## Notes

1 William Stanley Rubin, *"Primitivism" in 20th Century Art: Affinity of the Tribal and the Modern*, Vol. 1 (Museum of Modern Art, 1984). This important late twentieth-century show is critiqued in Jack D. Flam, *Primitivism and Twentieth-Century Art: A Documentary History* (2003). See also Naomi Sawelson-Gorse, *Women in Dada: Essays on Sex, Gender, and Identity* (1998).
2 Houston Baker, *Modernism and the Harlem Renaissance* (1989), 5.
3 William Francis Allen, Charles Pickard Ware, and Lucy McKim Garrison, *Slave Songs of the United States* (1867).
4 John Richardson, *A life of Picasso* (2007), 451.
5 Georgina Born, ed., *Western Music and Its Others: Difference, Representation, and Appropriation in Music* (2000).
6 Kurt Eisen, *Theatrical Ethnography and Modernist Primitivism in Eugene O'Neill and Zora Neale Hurston* (2008).
7 Berndt Ostendorf, "Subversive Reeducation? Jazz as a Liberating Force in Germany and Europe," in *Revue Francaise d'Etudes Américaines* (2001), 1–2.
8 Adam Gussow, "Racial Violence, 'Primitive' Music, and the Blues Entrepreneur: W. C. Handy's Mississippi Problem," *Southern Cultures* (Fall 2002), 56–77.
9 "'When Hearts Beat Like Native Drums:' Music and the Sexual Dimensions of the Notions of 'Savage' and 'Civilized' in Tarzan and His Mate, 1934," *Africa Today* (Winter 2001), 48, 4. 2001. Clara Henderson. pp. 113 and 97.
10 Harry Justin Elam, *African-American Performance and Theater History* (2001), 5, 101–2.
11 Maria Damon, "The Jewish Entertainer as Cultural Lightning Rod: The Case of Lenny Bruce," *Postmodern Culture* 7/2 (1997).
12 Sidney J. Lemelle, ed., *Imagining Home: Class, Culture, and Nationalism in the African Diaspora* (1994).
13 Kofi Agawu, "The Invention of African Rhythm," *Journal of the American Musicological Society* Vol. 48, No. 3 (Autumn, 1995), 388–395.

# Selected Bibliography


Apostolos-Cappadona, Diane. "Discerning the Hand of Fatima: An Iconological Investigation of the Role of Gender in Religious Art." In *Beyond the Exotic: Women's Histories in Islamic Societies*, Amira El-Azhary Sonbol (Ed.). Syracuse: Syracuse University Press, 2005.

Billington, James. "Bell and Cannon." In *The Icon and the Axe: An Interpretive History of Russian Culture*. New York: Vintage, 1970, 37–8.

Blake, Jody. *Le Tumulte Noir: Modernist Art and Popular Entertainment in Jazz-Age Paris, 1900–1930*. University Park, PA: Penn State University Press, 1999.

Blassingame, John. *The Slave Community: Plantation Life in the Antebellum South*. New York: Oxford University Press, 1972.

Boyd, Brian. *Vladimir Nabokov: The American Years*. Princeton: Princeton University Press, 1993.

Brooks, Daphne. "'All That You Can't Leave Behind': Black Female Soul Singing and the Politics of Surrogation in the Age of Catastrophe." *Meridians* 8/1 *Representin': Women, Hip Hop, and Popular Music* (2008), 180–204.

Burnim, Mellonee and Portia Maultsby (Eds.). *African American Music: An Introduction*. Abingdon, Oxon and New York: Routledge, 2006.

Campbell, Mary B. *The Witness and the Other World: Exotic European Travel Writing: 1400–1600*. American Council of Learned Societies. Ithaca, NY: Cornell University Press, 1991.

Caughie, Pamela. "Passing as Modernism." *Modernism/Modernity* 12/3 (2005), 385–406.

Chaney, Michael. "Slave Cyborgs and the Black Infovirus: Ishmael Reed's Cybernetic Aesthetics." *Modern Fiction Studies* 49/2 (2003), 261–83.

Chvaicer, Maya. "The Criminalization of Capoeira in Nineteenth century Brazil." *Hispanic American Historical Review* 82/3 (2002), 525–47.

Cohen, Michael. "Jim Crow's Drug War: Race, Coca Cola, and the Southern Origins of Drugs." *Southern Cultures* 12/3 (Fall 2006), 55–79.

Collins, Lisa. "Economies of Flesh: Representing the Black Female Body in Art." In *Skin Deep, Spirit Strong: The Black Female Body in American Culture*, Kimberly Gisele Wallace-Sanders (Ed.), Ann Arbor: University of Michigan Press, 2002.

Collinson, Francis. *The Bagpipe*. London: Routledge & Kegan Paul, 1975.

Corbould, Clare. "Streets, Sounds and Identity in Interwar Harlem." *Journal of Social History* 40 (Summer 2007), 861.

Cullen Rath, Richard. *How Early America Sounded*. Ithaca: Cornell University Press, 2005.

Debret, Jean Baptist. *Viagem Pitoresca e Histórica ao Brasil*. Paris: Firmin-Didot Fréres, 1834.

Dinnerstein, Joel. *Swinging the Machine: Modernity, Technology, and African American Culture*. Amherst: University of Massachusetts Press, 2003.

Dodds, Baby and Larry Gara. *The Baby Dodds Story*. Los Angeles: Contemporary Press, 1959.

Ellison, Ralph. *Invisible Man*. New York: Random House, 1952.

Emery, Lynne. *Black Dance in the United States from 1615 to 1970*. Princeton: Princeton University Press, 1972.

Epstein, Dena J. *Sinful Tunes and Spirituals: Black Folk Music to the Civil War*. Urbana and Chicago: University of Illinois Press, 1977, 2nd. 2003.

Foerstel, Herbert N. *Banned in the Media: A Reference Guide to Censorship in the Press*. Westport, CT: Greenwood Press, 1998.

Fox, Robert Elliot. *Masters of the Drum: Black Lit/Oratures across the Continuum*. Westport, CT: Greenwood Press, 1995.

Fryer, Peter. *Rhythms of Resistance: African Musical Heritage in Brazil*. London: Pluto Press, 2000.

Gilroy, Paul. *The Black Atlantic*. Cambridge, MA: Harvard University Press, 1993.

Grandt, Jürgen. *Kinds of Blue: The Jazz Aesthetic in African American Narrative*. Columbus, OH: Ohio State Press, 2004.

Holloway, Joseph. "Time in the African Diaspora: The Gullah Experience." In *Time in the Black Experience*, Joseph K. Adjaye (Ed.). Westport, CT: Greenwood Press, 1994.

Latrobe, Benjamin Henry Boneval. *Impressions Respecting New Orleans: Diary & Sketches, 1818–1820*. New York: Columbia University Press, 1951.

Lazaro, Albert. "James Joyce's Encounters with Spanish Censorship, 1939–1966." *Joyce Studies Annual* 12 (2001), 38–40.

Lyotard, Jean-Francois. "Simplifying to the Extreme, I Define Postmodern as Incredulity toward Metanarratives." *The Postmodern Condition* (1979), xxiv–xxv.

Maultsby, Portia and Mellonee Burnim (Eds.). *Issues in African American Music: Power, Gender, Race, Representation*. Abingdon, Oxon and New York: Routledge, 2016.

McCord, David J. (Ed.). "The Statutes at Large of South Carolina." In *Acts Relating to Charleston, Courts, Slaves, and Rivers*, Vol. 7. Columbia, SC: A. S. Johnston, 1840.

Menard, Louis. "Introduction to Edmund White, Memoirs of Hecate County." *New York Review of Books* (2004), xi.

Meyer, Michael A. *Tradition and Enlightenment, 1600–1780*, Vol. I *of German-Jewish History in Modern Times*. New York: Columbia University Press, 1996.

Montesinos Sale, Maggie. *The Slumbering Volcano: American Slave Ship Revolts and the Production of Violent Masculinities*. Durham, NC: Duke University Press, 1997.

Nelson Limerick, Patricia. *The Legacy of Conquest*. New York: W. W. Norton, 1987.

Nye, David. *Consuming Power: A Social History of American Energies*. Cambridge: MIT Press, 1999.

Okpewho, Isidore. "Walcott, Homer, and the 'Black Atlantic'." *Research in African Literature* 33/1 (Spring 2002), 27–44.

Olatunji, Babatunde. *The Beat of My Drum: An Autobiography*. Philadelphia: Temple University Press, 2005.

Perry, Imani. *Prophets of the Hood*. Durham, NC: Duke University Press, 2004.

Quilley, Geoff and Kay Dian Kriz (Eds.). *An Economy of Colour: Visual Culture and the North Atlantic World, 1660–1830*. Manchester, UK: Manchester University Press, 2003.

Raussert, William. *Negotiating Temporal Differences: Blues, Jazz and Narrativity in African American Culture*. Heidelberg: C. Winter, 2000.

Rawick, George P. (Ed.). *The Federal Writers' Project, The American Slave: A Composite Autobiography*, 22 vols. Westport, CT: Greenwood Press, 1972–1979.

Rodano, Ronald. "Soul Texts and the Blackness of Folk." *Modernism/Modernity* 2/1 (1995), 71–95.

Rodano, Ronald. "Narrating Black Music's Past." *Radical History Review* 84 (2002), 115–18.

Rucker, Walter. *The River Flows on: Black Resistance, Culture, and Identity Formation in Early America*. Baton Rouge: Louisiana State University Press, 2006.

Ryan, Mary. *Cradle of the Middle Class*. New York: Cambridge University Press, 1983.

Smith, Jeff. "Black Faces, White Voices: The Politics of Dubbing in Carmen Jones." *The Velvet Light Trap* 51 (2003), 29–42, 38.

Smith, Mark. "Producing Sense, Consuming Sense, Making Sense: Perils and Prospects for Sensory History." *Journal of Social History* 40/4 (2007), 841–58.

Southern, Eileen (Ed.). *Readings in Black American Music*. New York: W. W. Norton, 1971.

Southern, Eileen. *The Music of Black Americans: A History*. New York: W. W. Norton, 1997.

Southern, Eileen and Josephine Wright (Eds.). "African American Traditions in Song, Sermon Tale, and Dance, 1600s–1920." In *An Annotated Bibliography of Literature, Collections, and Artworks*. The Greenwood Encyclopedia of Black Music. Westport, CT: Greenwood, 1990.

Stuckey, Sterling. *Going through the Storm: The Influence of African American Art in History*. New York: Oxford University Press, 1993.

Szwed, John F. and Roger D. Abrahams. *Afro-American Folk Culture: An Annotated Bibliography of Materials from North, Central, and South America and the West Indies*. Philadelphia: Institute for the Study of Human Issues, 1978.

Van den Abbelle, Georges. "The Persecution of Writing: Revisiting Strauss and Censorship." Diacritics 27/2 (1997), 3.

Vlach, John Michael. *The Afro-American Tradition in Decorative Arts*. Cleveland: Cleveland Museum of Art, 1978. Reprint 1990 by Athens, GA and London: Brown Thrasher Books, The University of Georgia Press.

Weheliye, Alexander. "'Feenin': Posthuman Voices in Contemporary Black Popular Music." *Social Text* 20/2 (2002), 21–47.

White, Graham. *The Sounds of Slavery*. Boston: Beacon Press, 2006.

Wilcken, Lois. *Encyclopedia of Slave Resistance and Rebellion*, Rodriguez, Junius (Ed.). Westport, CT - London: Greenwood Press, 2007, 337–9.

Wilson, Sule Greg. *The Drummer's Path: Moving the Spirit with Ritual and Traditional Drumming*. Rochester, VT: Inner Traditions and Bear & Company, 1992.

# Index

For Product Safety Concerns and Information please contact our EU representative GPSR@taylorandfrancis.com
Taylor & Francis Verlag GmbH, Kaufingerstraße 24, 80331 München, Germany

www.ingramcontent.com/pod-product-compliance
Lightning Source LLC
LaVergne TN
LVHW010929110826
845149LV00013B/2520

* 9 7 8 1 0 3 2 2 4 0 0 9 1 *